PRAISE FOR *VISCERAL RESONANCE*

"Traditionally, physicians have been taught that suffering was something to be 'witnessed objectively' and then 'alleviated' through action. Using the theological perspective of Thomas Aquinas and approaches from narrative-based medicine, Dr. Ann Sirek offers a model of care that prioritizes the removal of obstacles to personal agency and flourishing. This approach incorporates the traditional need for medical meaning making, while honoring the practical knowledge that only the body and the five senses can provide, for both patient and healer. The possibility of transformation occurs through a 'visceral', embodied accompaniment. This book reminds us why theology should not be excluded from the company of bioethics and philosophy in our growing field of medical humanities."

—ALLAN PETERKIN, Professor of Psychiatry and Family Medicine and Head of the Program in Health, Arts, and Humanities, University of Toronto

"Dr. Sirek highlights the poverty of dealing with human suffering with only the traditional rational and detached scientific approach. She develops a model that is attuned to the personal story of sufferers, with their emotions, feelings, and experiences. This theological focus on the embodied and sensory nature of human experience is also applicable to other fields. In biblical studies, a narrative reading of texts with this sensitivity and awareness helps to unlock the deeper meaning of the symbols, images, and rhetoric."

—SCOTT M. LEWIS, SJ, Associate Professor of New Testament, Regis College, Toronto School of Theology

"Sirek re-visions the meaning of patient-centered practices for transformative healing by engaging a brilliant tapestry of voices from across disciplines in light of her own commitments and insights as a physician and theologian. Her rereading of Thomas Aquinas on the psychosomatic self invites and challenges all teachers and practitioners dedicated to authentic caregiving and healing to learn the praxis of sustained engagement with the experience of the sufferer as pathway to empowerment, wellness, and transformation."

—JENNIFER CONSTANTINE JACKSON, Director of Graduate Studies, Department of Theology and Religious Studies, Villanova University

"Ann Sirek uses Aquinas' understanding of the sensuality of human experience to gain a new perspective 'from below' on the condition of the sufferer precisely in her immobility, silences, and broken words. Sirek accompanies the sufferer as she gropes toward a self-narrative open to the spirit of resurrection and the freedom of movement it enables. She writes as both experienced physician and theological ethicist, offering fresh insight to medical clinicians and theological ethicists alike."

—ROBERT SWEETMAN, H. Evan Runner Chair in the History of Philosophy, Institute for Christian Studies, Toronto

"*Visceral Resonance* is an academically challenging work calling for an ethical shift in medical practice from the *view from the top* to a *view from the bottom*, an inversion supported by a Thomist perspective. It's written from compelling compassion that unwaveringly believes a new perspective is required to address suffering that can find flourishing and well-being beyond the presenting trial. Here you will find the heart of a physician and the mind of a theologian."

—GAILMARIE HENDERSON, Faculty, Thorneloe University, Sudbury, Ontario

Visceral Resonance

Visceral Resonance

A Theological Essay on Attending the Sufferer

ANN SIREK

Foreword by David B. Burrell, CSC

PICKWICK *Publications* · Eugene, Oregon

VISCERAL RESONANCE
A Theological Essay on Attending the Sufferer

Pickwick Publications
An Imprint of Wipf and Stock Publishers
199 W. 8th Ave., Suite 3
Eugene, OR 97401

www.wipfandstock.com

PAPERBACK ISBN: 978-1-7252-7250-7
HARDCOVER ISBN: 978-1-7252-7249-1
EBOOK ISBN: 978-1-7252-7251-4

Cataloguing-in-Publication data:

Names: Sirek, Ann, author. | Burrell, David B., foreword.

Title: Visceral resonance : a theological essay on attending the sufferer /
Ann Sirek ; foreword by David B. Burrell.

Description: Eugene, OR : Pickwick Publications, 2020 | Includes
bibliographical references and index.

Identifiers: ISBN 978-1-7252-7250-7 (paperback) | ISBN 978-1-7252-
7249-1 (hardcover) | ISBN 978-1-7252-7251-4 (ebook)

Subjects: LCSH: Suffering—Religious aspects—Christianity. | Thomas,
Aquinas, Saint, 1225?–1274.

Classification: BS680.S854 S61 2020 (paperback) | BS680.S854 S61 (ebook)

10/23/20

This book is dedicated to Diane Frederick, RN, my mentor and role model, and to Robert Liddy, CR, my first real friend.

Contents

List of Tables

Foreword

Given the author's extensive practice as a physician, as well as studied enculturation in Thomas Aquinas's approach to embodied human nature, her clarity of expression comes as no surprise, yet it is refreshingly salutary. Especially as she assimilates Thomas's reflections on our inherent "body-soul" composition to adopt a "view from below" in abiding contrast to an analytic perspective "from above" which cannot help but treat us in universal categories. Yet given her clinical humane perspective, Ann Sirek prefers the posture of "accompaniment" and finds it more respectful and admissive of human suffering. All this is articulated as she introduces her complementary approach at the outset of this inquiry. And so readers will find themselves accompanied as they are led into a fresh perspective for medical ethics.

As a bonus, health professionals and students of Aquinas will each be enlightened by this hybrid effort. For the very task of showing how such apparently diverse approaches can be mutually illuminating offers refreshment to our world of specialization—and is that not the lifeblood of ethics, and notably theological ethics? Yet this disarmingly straightforward inquiry belies that academic descriptor by inviting us to accompany the author's interior transformation, presaging a shift in our very selves as well as a fresh perspective on the subject. We are invited into explicitly religious discourse to supplement the more technical idiom familiar to either scientific or theological treatments. So, the invitation can be a challenge as well. *Caveat lector.*

David B. Burrell, CSC
March 12, 2020

Acknowledgments

I am grateful to all the unnamed patients who have passed through my hands. From their trust in me I learned to step out of my intellectual seat as the clinical observer and to resonate physically with them as fellow human beings who simply wanted to feel well again. From my doctor-parents and from my clinician-mentors I learned that to embrace not only the science but also this medical art of caring for the sick is to live a good and honorable life.

In the academy, where a doctor's experience is neither readily perceived nor easily received, the support of Robert Sweetman, my doctoral thesis director, was invaluable. He initiated me into the learned language of peaceable interlocution.

I am also indebted to John English, SJ, Jack Milan, and Alexandra Caverly Lowery, who companioned my soul's gradual transformation from moral marching into a creative, cosmic dancing.

I am grateful to my children and grandchildren for their unfailing love.

Abbreviations

ST   Thomas Aquinas. *Summa Theologica*. Translated by Fathers of the English Dominican Province. Complete English ed. 5 vols. Notre Dame, IN: Ave Maria, 1920.

Introduction

This theological essay on attending the sufferer is an articulation of a heuristic arising from the cross-fertilization of my professional experience as a physician observing human beings who suffer and my doctoral research into the *Summa Theologiae* of Thomas Aquinas on the nature of human corporeality. The prevailing perspective—the view from above—engages a heuristic based upon statements of universal truths. In moral philosophy and theology, including practical ethics, we think in terms of the universally true; we want to distinguish between right and wrong *based upon the truth* of the matter. In the health sciences, pursuit of the true proceeds according to our abstract models of biological systems, which define normal physiology and the pathological deviant from such norms; in science, normal has perhaps become a surrogate marker for the true. These approaches based upon a pursuit of the true are powerful because intellectually sophisticated and logically persuasive. I would suggest, however, that this prevailing heuristic of logic in search of the truth excludes certain aspects of a sufferer's reality. I propose to articulate a complementary heuristic better suited to attending a sufferer. The proposed approach is complementary to the questing for the true; it involves a questing for the good, not always the true good, but the best possible under the circumstances. I will refer to this approach as the perspective from below.

The approach from above, so characteristic of modernity, takes the familiar form of the subject-object paradigm: the dispassionate observer is empowered to intervene. The objectified and vulnerable sufferer becomes a passive recipient, a passivity that comes uncomfortably close to loss of agency. On this view, the experience of the sufferer is abstracted and cognized as "suffering." Working with suffering-as-idea, the dispassionate agency of intervention draws upon norms and universals that may unintentionally alter the experiential reality of the sufferer and eclipse its validity. For this reason, an alternate heuristic suggests itself, one in which the experience remains particular and is not "squashed" into a model or a statement of the universal. When we "squash" a person's experience of suffering into the form of a universal, we are effectively losing the voice of the sufferer and privileging the voice of the observer. Experience "morphs" from vulnerability to culpability when the sufferer internalizes the perspective of the observer and critically analyzes (adjudicates) the suffering self. Suffering thus distorted becomes a datum for empirical observation. The proposed view from below retains the *experience* of suffering as a felt-sense within the corporeal sensory nature, indeed, in the very particularity of the sufferer's own sensory nature. It is this felt experience of the sensory corporeality, in all its particularity, that compels the proposed approach from below.

In the first chapter, human corporeality according to Thomas Aquinas (*Summa Theolgiae*) will provide a model that serves as an alternate to modernity's sciences, i.e., physiology, psychology, and the respective pathologies. Thomas observes that living bodies desire being, indeed well-being, not harm and not annihilation. No different than any other living being, human beings in their sensory nature are possessed of primal movements towards the good and out of harm's way. It is this movement towards the good away from evil—advancing towards flourishing/emerging from suffering—that serves as a theoretical foundation for the proposed new heuristic around attending the sufferer. The pursuit of the true and the true good will be bracketed off temporarily in the interest of understanding the human process around pursuit of the best possible move at this particular time under the circumstances. A human

being arrives at flourishing by a stepwise series of such best possible moves in the context of one's personal history of experienced
(i.e., corporeally imprinted) hurts and delights. Flourishing may
be understood as a surrogate term for the good (the best possible
under the circumstances), a good described not in the speculative
terms of universal truths, but in terms of particular experiences of
the not-so-good. Thus, as Thomas suggested, pursuit of the good is
suitably juxtaposed with avoidance of evil. The movement towards
good, away from evil, is the movement of advance towards flourishing, which, when viewed from below, is experienced as the emergence from suffering. These aspects of the sensory human nature,
adapted from the *Summa Theologiae* of Thomas Aquinas, will serve
as a theoretical foundation for the new ethics discourse to be specified in the subsequent chapters.

In the second chapter, the importance of movement and its
hindrance are examined, deriving understanding from such experiences as bondage and freedom, silencing and voicing, immobility
and vitality, victim and agent, and so on. A discourse of movement
has its own rationality, distinct from deductive and empirical approaches. A discourse of movement takes shape when one's focus
rests upon the sensory corporeal nature, allowing cognition to go
out of focus and movement to come into sharp definition. By contrast, when the sensory nature is examined through the lens of the
intellectual nature with its cognitions and abstract speculations, felt
experience is conflated with abstract cognitions, which blurs the
sensing, human corporeality, with its particularities and subjectivities. What we are after is clarity around the movement of emergence
from suffering into flourishing, and such clarity comes through an
exploration of the corporeal sensing of harm and wellbeing. In order to perceive the rationality of dynamic sensory nature, one must
avoid conflating it with the logic of the discursive aspect of intellectual nature. I will show that the rationality of the sensory nature
is found in its movements.

In the third chapter, the analytic logic of the discursive intellectual nature (suited to the subject-object dualism or cause-effect-
intervention paradigms of science) is contrasted with the storied
rationality of the sensing, feeling, moving sensory nature (suited to

the dynamic of emergence from suffering into flourishing). Storied thinking is not just any old story. In the context of attending the sufferer the point is the ontologic potential of the narrative. When storied thinking is ordered to healing and restoring vital energies, there is intentional attentiveness to the ineffable and the human potential to participate Divine Being. The Divine Being of Christian tradition is pure *actus,* movement, vitality, or dynamism; in such Being there is no death at all, only an infinite fullness of living movement. Stories that heal through participation in Divine Aliveness have particular characteristics. They are spoken in the voice of the first person, the sufferer, and not in the third person voice of the observer. The voice of the first person expresses experiences of vulnerability, not adjudications of culpability. Such narratives of suffering extend over time, often over a life-time. They narrate subjectivity and particularity. They grope for a language that exposes the felt sensory experiences that arise from particular circumstances by using linguistic forms such as metaphor and symbolism. Storied rationality is a moral desiring for the good—for something better—that comes about in the process of the telling. In the process of the telling moral agency is born.

In the fourth chapter, I draw a contrast between a particular example of misery (suffering) viewed from above through the language of analytical logic and the same circumstances viewed from below through the power of symbol. When we view/observe from above, the sensations within the body are sanitized out and rendered disembodied cognitions. When we view from below, experiences remain in the body as felt sensations; this is important at the level of moral agency for both teller and listener. While the teller experiences an immersion into his/her own felt sensory experience of some particular hurtful circumstance, the listener vicariously experiences those gut feelings with the teller. This visceral resonance preserved as experience, without being psychologized or analyzed into abstract cognitions, affords the movement or corporeal dynamic of progression, advance, emergence, transformation, and so on. To progress from suffering towards flourishing is a mystery that calls forth its own kind of linguistic idiom, namely, the use of symbol and metaphor. Such progression is to participate the ineffable, divine *actus* or movement. Divine movement is eternally donative of life; the divine creative act does not include annihilation. In the Christian tradition it is the resurrection narratives as well as the stories of Christ's birth, life, suffering, and death that give expression to the primal human longing for release from annihilating states of bondage and immobilization into ultimate vitality. Such narratives are not for the critical intellect; they work from below as symbols expressing the experiences and longings of our human corporeality. Thus understood, the symbol embedded in narrative becomes a kind of linguistic method that mediates the graced transformation from suffering to flourishing.

The purpose of this four-part essay is to sketch out an approach to moral agency in the face of suffering that avoids imperatives of power over another because such imperatives risk inadvertently aggravating the other's suffering. I am proposing a shift in perspective. The proposed new perspective is called the view from below. On this view, the emphasis falls upon the sufferer, who tells of experiences that have hindered his flourishing, that have paralyzed her capacity for agency, that have hurt his soul, that have adjudicated her vulnerability as culpability. On this view, there is the additional shift in emphasis away from the universally true principles towards the good—the best possible move for now under the circumstances. Cognition towards the true and movement towards the good are retained as *distinct* capacities. The underlying presumption is that the corporeality, at a primal level, moves according to a longing to feel well and a revulsion to being harmed. Although together they comprise a whole, the sensing, feeling corporeality is not to be conflated with the intellectual nature of immaterial cognitions and abstractions. This underlying presumption, extrapolated from the *Summa* of Thomas Aquinas, becomes a foundation for the moral project of attending the sufferer. The modern, scientific truths of physiology, psychology, sociology, etc. have their place when the goal is intervention, but attending the sufferer calls forth a different paradigm, one that is rooted in a more ancient understanding of human nature and its susceptibility to being hurt.

The reader for whom I write is the academic who has inherited the perspective from above; the theologian who thinks like a philosopher will be enriched by a complementary perspective. The contextual theologian may also find relevance in this perspective from below; context is perhaps a synonym for the dynamic gradient that moves from suffering towards flourishing, i.e., the view from below. The clinical ethicist who struggles for a language with which to justify companioning a sufferer who appears to be at odds with abstract statements of morality will hopefully find the proposed linguistic framework helpful. And finally, I harbor the humble hope that my physician colleagues, especially those who probe their own spiritual traditions, might also find in these pages something to revitalize their own souls, so easily rendered mute and paralyzed by the relentless logic of interventional medicine.

1

The Dynamic Body, according to
Thomas Aquinas

In this first chapter I will sketch out an understanding of human nature that will ground the medical, the pastoral, and indeed the personal art of attending the sufferer. I write for those whose concern for the sufferer—the impoverished widow, the lost orphan, the disenfranchised foreigner of Scripture—centers around a questing for the truth; I wish to flesh out that truth by an exploration of the dynamics of human corporeality. Just as the medical professional uses physiology to ground her approach, the theologian often uses philosophy to ground his hermeneutic. What I propose to do is to use my firsthand experience (as a physician) in the medical art of attending the sufferer as a lead into the theology, and then to use the selected theological texts to further illumine the approach to a particular sufferer. I want to articulate an understanding of human nature as illumined by theology, rather than understanding the human body scientifically as illumined by physiology. In medicine, the artful practice of attending the sufferer is currently taught by drawing upon the humanities such as history, literature, the performing arts, and the visual arts, as well as by explorations in philosophy and spirituality. The exploration of theology as a resource for the art of attending the sufferer has been hindered perhaps by a bias of modernity that upholds an opposition between religion and science. Such a wide variety of resources, as well as the built-in biases of modernity, lead to the question, "Can one identify a unifying heuristic undergirding the art of attending the sufferer?"

My intention is to flesh out this question and begin a conversation, both scholarly and practical, around the fundamental aspects of our approach to suffering and, even more importantly, our approach to the sufferer. It is to the medieval Christian tradition and specifically to the scholarship of Thomas Aquinas that I now turn, mindful that the hospitals and hospices of contemporary Western cultures have their origins in the monasteries of medieval Christian Europe. I have chosen to explore the European Christian tradition because it is the tradition of my ancestors, a tradition in which I was raised. I am not naïve to the hurt and harm left in the wake of Christendom and its colonialist strategies. It is not the politics that I wish to explore but rather the wisdom of the tradition around suffering; there might be (and indeed I think there is) something worth transposing into the context of the post-modern sufferer. In this vein then, it is my sincere hope that readers might feel invited and inspired to explore their own religious/spiritual traditions to discover the aspect of meaning in birth, life, suffering, death, and after-life. Such explorations will enable a broader conversation and perhaps a renewed wisdom in how we care for the sick and the suffering—and for ourselves.

I begin with an anecdote to illustrate the not infrequent tension between a professional's intent to follow evidence-based, clinical guidelines and the sufferer's agenda of healing and wellness. An Indigenous woman once challenged my approach to her diabetes: "Why are you doing all this to me? I don't want it!" It was an awkward moment in which I realized that my efforts to teach her home blood glucose monitoring and dietary carbohydrate awareness had not been perceived as helpful. My intuition was that her succinct exclamation was less about diabetes and more about her sensed victim identity. Her initial presence had been difficult—mute, passive, and angry—and I had intentionally focused upon the measurable outcomes of her diabetes management. But she, the sufferer, was finding her voice and insisting upon my attention. She was undergoing some sort of identity shift, which, though awkward for me, was potentially a movement of emergence out of her past bondage toward a freedom for flourishing. In order to be present and attentive to her process, I required more insight into this human dynamic of emergence from suffering into flourishing. There was something required of me that was quite distinct from the competent management of her diabetes; in fact, I had to temporarily suspend the practice of scientific medicine in order to allow her experience of suffering to come into focus. "What would it be like if you considered diabetes care as something *you do for yourself*?" I suggested rather tentatively. But this capacity to "do for yourself" is easier said than done; it becomes part of the healing process. And healing is an experience that (arguably) may fall more into the domain of the human spirit than into the domain of physiology-gone-wrong. This chapter (and indeed this book) is about healing in terms of the domain of the human spirit—embodied.

Thomas Aquinas writes about the spiritual journey with a perspective that, although perhaps privileging the working of the intellect and the will (the view "from above"), does offer a detailed account of the structure and dynamism of the material (i.e., corporeal), sensory nature. My way of reading Thomas Aquinas is a kind of scanning for the experience of sensory nature as it undergoes a transformation of ever-increasing vitality toward the *telos* of a beatific, eternal resting in God. This emphasis upon the sensory aspect of human nature (the body) will be called the view "from below." My method is to *extrapolate* the insights of Thomas so that a rigour begins to emerge around the art of attending corporeal suffering. Schooled in the analytical ways of science, the critical mind of modernity, (including the clinical mind), has perhaps acquired an unfortunate bias that overlooks the innate intelligence of the sensory corporeality. To this end, the medieval paradigm is helpful: our modern, default heuristic of analysis, diagnostics, and therapeutics comes into focus as a bias. Not wrong, but just one of many ways to view the world. I intentionally avoid approaching suffering in terms of psychology, sociology, and biology; science has already been done in fine scholarly tradition. I propose a perspective that views suffering as an evil or a stumbling block, which besets one like an illness, hindering one's progress toward flourishing and well-being. I position suffering as that starting point from which the fallen (meaning vulnerable, not bad) human being must work out a differentiated and particular emergence into personal flourishing. This pursuit of flourishing and vitality—that is, the fullness of being—is a process that involves a progressive integration of all aspects of one's human nature. Note that when viewed from above, the sensory and the intellectual natures are seen ideally as an integrity or hylomorphic unity. But from below, we see the fallen state in which that integrity, in some particular way for each person, has become broken; there are capacities that have become immobilized or silenced in the wake of some particular experience of evil (harm or hurt). Imprints of evil-as-hurt exist in each person-as-sufferer, and those imprints, according to the Christian tradition, are healable and transformable. When I was ready to see my patient as a sufferer rather than as a diabetic, I could then also see her sensory nature coming alive with the arduous passions of anger, fear, and hope. Just as I had to bracket off her diabetes for the time being, the reader must understand that in writing this essay, I am bracketing off the prevailing view from above, in which the sensory nature, with its experiences of suffering and flourishing, is understood in terms of abstract conceptualizations. My intention is to focus upon the *experience* (rather than the abstract concepts) of suffering and transformation as I work towards a foundation for the art of attending suffering.

In this first chapter I will build my position in three stages. First, I will outline the kinds of movements that Thomas Aquinas describes in the sensory nature: apprehension of, appetition toward, and finally abiding in the good. Second, I will offer a descriptive definition of "suffering" as a hindrance to these sensory movements in pursuit of the good. Finally, I will submit that the higher intelligence called practical reason is distinct from speculative reason in that it works directly with the sensory nature's orientation to avoid being harmed and to advance towards flourishing.

These elements, outlined in the first chapter, will be further elaborated in the subsequent chapters towards proposing a theological foundation for attending the sufferer, a foundation that is not in the analytical mind but has its locus in the felt visceral sensations of our human corporeality. Moreover, the elements highlighted in this first chapter will call forth a distinctive kind of discourse, which will complement and enrich the traditional principles of morality and the modern cause-effect models of disease.

THE SENSORY NATURE AND ITS MOVEMENT

I begin with a description of movement as intrinsic to being human and to being alive. For Thomas, things that are alive *move*, and such things can also *be moved* like inanimate objects. Moreover, he describes death in terms of an absence of life's vital movements: "When it no longer has any movement of itself, but is only moved by another power, then its life is said to fail, and the animal to be dead."[1] Importantly, Thomas notes that to live "is not an accidental but an essential predicate."[2] By contrast, to understand is an accidental predicate of being, similar to the predicates to eat, grow, reproduce, and move (walk, run, crawl, swim, fly) from one place to another. Human beings move like animals towards that which provides the pleasure of satiety, growth, and health. The primal pursuit of such pleasures ensures safety from harm and the freedom to survive and indeed to flourish. Human beings, unlike animals,[3] can revise their movements according to past experiences of pleasure and hurt. In other words, there is an intelligence unique to the

1. ST I.18.1. It is noteworthy that Thomas offers a non-scientific description of life—sheer being and wellness. The modern definition of life in terms of death reflects the contemporary penchant for empirical reality. Thomas enables the modern reader to set aside this preoccupation with empirical realities and to grope beyond them towards a broader understanding of suffering and wellness.

2. ST I.18.2.

3. For example, a dog will eat garbage again and again despite the (painful?) bowel upset brought about by eating garbage. A dog does not modify its behavior according to its experience.

human sensory nature that confers rationality upon human movement, and this intelligence is not the instinct that guides animal movement. Nor is it an intelligence of the analytical mind:

> By natural instinct . . . [animals] move themselves in respect to an end . . . apprehended by sense. [But human beings move according to] an end they themselves propose. . . . This can only be done by reason and intellect; whose province it is to know the proportion between the end and the means to that end, and duly coordinate them.[4]

Thomas would appear to be distinguishing between the "reason" of sensory nature and the "intellect" of intellectual nature. In a human being the movement that knows to get out of harm's way and advance towards wellbeing is neither animal instinct nor analytic intellect. Some sort of innate "smarts" differentiate between the bad (hurt/harm) and the good (wellbeing/flourishing) and give rise to the human being's movement at any given moment. The movements that arise from this innate capacity of sensory nature are called apprehension (sensory information goes in) and appetition (movement goes out). There is one other movement to be noted when considering the sensory nature. Human beings experience *being moved* by the divine principle of life. In other words, sensed movement can be an experience of participating divine vitality.[5] This being-moved makes possible the movement of resting in the good attained, being shaped, as it were, by the embrace of the good. When the sensory nature rests, attentive and responsive, the movement of contemplation is accomplished.

I will now elaborate upon each of these three movements of the sensory nature.

Apprehension is the movement whereby the alluring object enters from the exteriority into the interiority of the human agent. The external object is perceived by the familiar five senses of sight, touch, taste, hearing, and smell; there are also the important interior senses of imagination, memory, and cogitative sense. An external object or experience becomes imprinted upon the interiority in

4. ST I.18.3.
5. ST I.18.3.2.

the form of an image, or phantasm, that becomes the substrate, as it were, for the imagination and the memory. These images are not neutral photographs; they carry primal meanings of harm or good by virtue of the cogitative sense. Diana Fritz Cates puts it thus: "it is common for humans to judge a long thin object moving quickly through the grass at their feet to be a threat of some kind, even before they have time to think, 'this is a snake, and some snakes are dangerous.'"[6] The cogitative sense is a primal knowing capacity *of the body*. For Thomas, this is the locus of intersection of sensory and rational capacities, which he refers to as both the cogitative *sense* and the particular *reason*. Robert Miner interprets Thomas thus: "The particular reason is the capacity to arrive at estimations of utility or danger by associating sensible forms, neutral in them-selves, with stored images that are charged with pleasure or pain. As such it presupposes the imagination."[7] The apprehensive capacities of the sensory nature work together to configure imprints upon the sensory interiority that Thomas refers to as an *intentio*. The *intentiones* become important determinants of particular instances of appetitive movement. Elizabeth Anscombe has described intention as concealed within the interiority, revealed only in answer to the question, "Why did you do that?" Yet the intention of one's interior-ity need not be conceptual, as in the truth of an idea or principle. Intention, at the sensory level, has to do with desire or wanting:

> The conceptual connexion between "wanting" and "good" can be compared to the conceptual connexion between "judgment" and "truth." Truth is the object of judgment and good the object of wanting; it does not follow from this that everything wanted must be good.[8]

The movement of sensory apprehension has the good as its object; something that holds a promise of wellness has come up on the ra-dar of the sensory interiority. Note that the radar of sensory nature does not distinguish between a true or a false good.

---

6. Cates, *Aquinas on Emotions*, 114.

7. Miner, *Thomas Aquinas on the Passions*, 78.

8. Anscombe, *Intention*, 76.

Appetition is the second movement of the sensory nature. Arising from apprehension, it is movement that becomes apparent in the surrounding exteriority as a particular act or comportment. It is the movement of advancing towards a desirable object. The view from below, which sees the movements of the sensory nature unfiltered by the intellectual nature, understands appetition in terms of the passions. The passions are "the movements of the soul . . . disturbances rather than disease."[9] Although of the immaterial soul, these movements are at the same time corporeal experiences, or a "bodily transmutation," when something desirable and good is lost.[10] Hence sorrow and love are the concupiscible passions, sorrow more so than love. Anger, for example, is an irascible passion, and its physicality is described as "a kindling of the blood about the heart."[11] Courage, fear, despair, and hope are the other irascible passions. These passions of sensory nature, though potentially modulated by the higher capacities, arise independently of the intellect. Though potentially refined by the intellectual capacities, the sensory nature is vulnerable[12] to alluring objects in the external milieu, some of which may be experienced in the end as hurtful objects whose allure turns out to be deceptive. It is of importance to note that the passions are both a disturbance of the *immaterial* soul as well as movements of our sensory, *material* corporeality; the passions are not cognitions of intellectual nature but are a response within the sensory nature to experiences of hurt (evil) and wellbeing (the good)[13] On this view, the common contemporary translation of *passiones* as emotions may reflect our modern preoccupation with cognition, departing from what Thomas observed to be the functional human binary of cognition and movement.

Abiding in the good attained is the third movement of sensory nature. There is an experience of satiety and pleasure in arriving at union with the good. Conversely, there is an experience

9. ST I-II.22.2.

10. ST I-II.22.2.

11. ST I-II.22.2.3.

12. I use "vulnerable" to cohere with the Latin, *passio*, meaning to undergo or to be a passive recipient—of the good or of the not-so-good. See ST I-II.22.1

13. ST I-II.22.2.3.

of anxiety, frustration, despondency, and helplessness when that union proves to be an immersion in that which is hurtful and in that which obstructs wellbeing (the good). The movement of abiding in experiences of the good or the hurt is like an embrace to which the self contours itself. An embrace of hurt and harm shapes the self as sufferer while an embrace of wellness and health enables the self to flourish. When suffering comes about on account of human vulnerability to things that harm and obstruct our wellbeing, the speculative, problem-solving intellect may similarly be disoriented by mendacity and not know what to do. In the context of such suffering, the physical practice of intentional contemplative abiding in experiences of (divine) justice and mercy, both recollected and imagined, may afford the self a rising visceral awareness around how to move forward. In concert with the internal senses of memory and imagination, the cogitative sense/particular reason distinguishes between what hurts and what feels good, and from this experiential knowing a growing conviction takes shape around which part of one's circumstances is no longer coherent with justice and mercy. In other words, certain aspects of one's situation come into focus as no longer desirable or indeed as intolerable, triggering the passions of revulsion, courage, strength, and hope. Then, from these passions arise comportments of change. The act of contemplation of divine mercy and justice gradually brings about a new (graced) vitality and creativity to displace the previous bondage of immobility and muteness, enabling the sufferer to begin advancing towards wellness and flourishing. Without this contemplative movement of abiding in divine justice and mercy with attention to one's own particular narrative of hurt, the possibility of sensory nature leading the way forward is occluded by the frantic, futile attempts of a mind ordered exclusively to speculative problem-solving.

A DESCRIPTIVE DEFINITION OF SUFFERING

Having outlined the sensory nature as three distinct movements that, in concert, effect the emergence from harm and the advance toward flourishing, I will now elaborate briefly on a description of suffering in terms of this movement. "Suffering" is a modern word, which Thomas did not use. Moreover, different people seem to mean different things when they use the term "suffering." For example, the difficult, irascible passions are often understood as painful emotions, which become conflated with suffering. According to our cultural presumptions, there is a moral imperative to intervene in suffering, including psychological suffering. The science of psychology represents what I am calling the perspective from above, whereby suffering is understood in terms of a subject matter to be analyzed toward a solution. By contrast, when suffering is understood in terms of the sensory nature and its movements, then anger, fear, despair, and sorrow, as well as hope, joy, and delight are understood as experiences of sensory movement. Thomas called these movements "corporeal transmutations." On this view, the moral imperative becomes a process of ordering and shaping these movements so that the sufferer, like my angry patient, assumes progressive agency in the personal movement of emergence from evil into flourishing; the agency valued by my patient had nothing to do with the autonomous, independent self-management of her disease.

As I have indicated above, human nature is permeable not only to the good but also to the hurts that hinder the attainment of the good. Such hurt or hindrance can shape the apprehensive as well as the appetitive movements of the sensory nature. Dorothee Soelle describes the paralysis of the apprehensive sensory nature thus:

> [Apathy] is understood as a social condition in which people are so dominated by the goal of avoiding suffering that it becomes a goal to avoid human relationships and contacts altogether. In so far as the experiences of suffering . . . are repressed, there is a corresponding disappearance of passion for life and of the strength and intensity of its joys.[14]
>
> People stand before suffering like those who are colour-blind, incapable of perception, and without any sensibility. The consequence of this suffering-free state of well-being is that people's lives become frozen solid. Nothing threatens any longer, nothing grows any longer,

---

14. Martel, *High Mountains of Portugal,* 36.

with the characteristic pains that all growth involves, nothing changes. . . . [The] life curve flattens out completely so that even joy and happiness can no longer be experienced intensely.[15]

This description of apathy strikes me as complementary to Thomas's description of the paralysis of the appetitive sensory nature in the presence of overwhelming evil.

> The proper effect of sorrow consists in a certain "flight of the appetite." Wherefore the foreign element in the effect of sorrow, may be taken so as to affect the first part only, by excluding flight: and thus we have "anxiety" which weighs on the mind, so as to make escape seem impossible: . . . If, however, the mind be weighed down so much, that even the limbs become motionless, which belongs to "torpor," then we have the foreign element affecting both, since there is neither flight, nor is the effect in the appetite. And the reason why torpor especially is said to deprive one of speech is because of all the external movements the voice is the best expression of the inward thought and desire, not only in men, but also in other animals, as is stated in Polit. i,1.[16]

In colloquial parlance we might say that a person experiencing a threat to the self exhibits "fight, flight, or freeze." The passions of anger/courage might correspond to "fight," and fear to "flight." When the threat is overwhelming, torpor or the "freeze" mode takes over; all movement is gone, and the appearance of immobility or paralysis prevails. The only behaviors possible now are reflexive, robotic movements in response to some overwhelming power or command; such behaviors no longer reflect any real moral agency.

Yann Martel, in his novel, *The High Mountains of Portugal*, offers a description that would appear to illustrate behavior arising from these most profound states of apathy and torpor. His character Tomàs is on the journey of a sufferer, questing to make some sense of it all. In the archives of the museum where he works, Tomàs

---

15. Soelle, *Suffering*, 38–39.
16. ST I-II.35.8.

has found an ancient notebook, the personal diary of a missionary priest travelling through Africa with the intention of ministering to the slaves. Tomàs often takes inspiration from this diary. On one occasion he reads the priest's description of the slaves.

> Today I saw a fight on a plantation. Two slaves clashed. Others stood about with stupefied expressions. A female slave, the object of contention, looked on, impassive, indifferent. Whoever won, she would lose. Continually . . . the two fought, at first with words [and] gestures, then their fists, then their tools. The matter proceeded swiftly, from injured bodies, from bruising and bleeding to frenzied hacking, til the end was reached: a dead slave with a torso cleft with deep cuts [and] a half-severed head. Whereupon the other slaves, the female included, turned [and] got back to their work lest the overseer arrive on the scene. The victor slave, his visage apathetic, threw some soil on the body, then returning to cutting cane. None of the slaves will come forward to acknowledge or to explain, to accuse or defend. Just silence [and] the hoeing of sugar cane.[17]

In theological terms, what the priest had witnessed was sufferers who had been robbed of moral agency on account of oppression by an overlord with absolute control. Their humanity all but extinguished, they had become human beings reduced to sheer bestial violence. Although culpability for murder might be obvious here, I would complexify the picture by drawing attention to the vulnerability of these slaves. The very corporeality of the slaves had been permeated and imprinted with the cruelty of the overlords. Their acts were reduced to rote, knee-jerk type reactions that reflected an interiority shaped by violent cruelty.[18] The slaves were silent. Or more accurately, they had been silenced. Moreover, they were paralyzed and no longer able to engage the imagination towards more creativity of comportment. With their "stultified expressions," "his

17. Martel, *High Mountains of Portugal*.

18. I am following Soelle here. She describes three stages of suffering, the deepest being a state arising from experiences of overwhelming oppression, where behaviors are exclusively reactive. See Soelle, *Suffering*, 73.

visage apathetic," and the mindless, mechanical hoeing of the cane, the slaves were displaying the torpor and the apathy identified by both Aquinas and Soelle. This state of torpor and apathy, which I interpret as the shutting down of the apprehensive sensibilities and the appetitive passions, will serve as a theological definition for suffering. In the context of the suffering sensory nature, moral agency is silenced and paralyzed causing culpability to be mitigated by vulnerability, even while the imperative against murder remains true.[19]

PRACTICAL REASON AND THE SENSORY NATURE

When the view is from below and the focus is upon vulnerability, permeability, and sensibilities of the apprehensive capacity of sensory nature then one may better understand that the appetitions (manifested as acts, comportment, and behaviors) are arising from an interior matrix that is very complex indeed. In other words, apprehended experiences of harm (suffering) and of good (wellness) manifest in the world as related comportments; the slave, whose consciousness is shaped by annihilating experiences, kills. Experiences manifest as corresponding types of behavior. To make sense of a particular behavior requires attention to the non-syllogistic yet rational pursuit of survival, pleasure, and wellness of being. A human being knows at a primal level to move out of harm's way towards safety, satiety, and pleasurable experiences. The view from above would adjudicate the killing in terms of *culpability* for wrongdoing. But from below, the focus comes to rest upon the killer's *vulnerability* to annihilation by the master; that murderous slave, imprinted and shaped by endless experiences of repetitive annihilation, simply perpetrated more of the same.

Lived experiences of harm and good aggregate with experience, becoming increasingly nuanced through the practice of prudence. The virtue of prudence enables the know-how of practical

---

19. Gondreau, *Passions of Christ's Soul*. This author examines Aquinas on the passions of Christ, which research enables an appreciation of human vulnerability as contrasted with human culpability. In the fullness of his humanity, Christ was not culpable, but he certainly was vulnerable.

reason to aggregate around the good.[20] Practical reason is classified as a "higher" rationality whose work is to lead a primal movement in pursuit of the good (wellness) and in avoidance of evil (harm).[21] Something in the experiential sensory nature calls forth a certain rationality that is more than the particular reason of the cogitative sense. Moreover, this rationality called forth by sensory nature is distinct from the discursive, syllogistic logic that we understand as the dominant capacity of intellectual nature. The rationality that complements syllogistic logic and that is called forth by the cogitative sense/particular reason is referred to as practical reason in Thomas's text on natural law.[22] In the paragraphs below, I will articulate some aspects of practical reason according to Thomas.

It is important to the view from below to distinguish between syllogistic rationality and practical reason. Because the prevailing view is from above and all functions and capacities are classified according to the speculative intellect, this distinction has been controversial for the scholarly academy (theology and philosophy). In support of the view from below, Martin Rhonheimer has argued that the naturally rational—that is, practical reason—is not a subcategory of theoretical reasoning. Practical reason arises from a synthesis of past experiences of good and harm with the end or goal of some particular movement of advance towards flourishing (good) and emergence from harm (evil). Pursuit of the *truth* of the matter at hand is not the work of practical reason, although information about universal true and false premises may inform the particular movement. In other words, practical reason, when viewed "from below," is not the intelligence of logical deliberation but is rather that which impels movement of the sensory nature toward a particular good and away from a particular harm. Rhonheimer puts it thus,

> [Practical reason] has nothing to do with the question
> of derivation of judgements for concrete actions from

20. Prudence is the first of the four cardinal virtues; its work is the perfection of (practical) reason in pursuit of the good (ST I-II.61.2).

21. ST I-II.94.2.

22. ST I-II.94.

general norms [or principles], nor with maintaining an
infallibility of the prudent person in determining what
is "right" in every instance. What is meant is not factual
rectitude, but rather the moral "being right" or "being
good" of action on the basis of "practical truth," that is,
its coincidence with the goal of virtue.[23]

Practical experience around what feels hurtful and what feels good
does not depend for its verity upon syllogistic reasoning. Practical
reason is a distinct sort of knowing, perhaps better referred to as
"know-how." When viewed from below, the allure that an object
exerts and the shape of the arising movement is understood vis à vis
the experience of hurt or pleasure that dwells within, without *necessarily* engaging the argued and proven truth of the matter. Movement follows a gradient of hurt and pleasure, not true and false.
Hence the vulnerability of human nature: it is susceptible to the
attraction of a good that may turn out, in truth, to be not-so-good.
On Rhonheimer's view, Aquinas understands the sensory nature to
be following a law of nature, i.e., the law of allure and revulsion—
towards the good and away from the harmful.

Thus understood, this natural law is not a juridical process of
analytic adjudication and disabling penalty. Those who would conflate the movement principles of practical reason with the universal
statements of speculative reason are critiqued by Rhonheimer.:

> Honnefelder appears to conceive of the highest prin-
> ciple of the practical reason as a "statement" that "says"
> something, a binding expression, in fact. But when we
> consider it closely, neither the highest principle of the
> practical reason nor all consequent principles can be
> called "sentences" or "normative statements"; they can
> only become such in the mode of reflection of reason
> upon its own practical act. The principles of the practical
> reason (precepts of natural law) are those first practi-
> cal judgments, which through being embedded in the
> appetitive dynamism of the natural inclinations have a
> fundamentally practical/moving character, and as such,
> independently of linguistic formulation, they first of all

23. ST I-II.95–128.

constitute the subject as an acting subject through its
orientation toward the naturally known good.[24]

The human capacity to respond with the passions of sensory nature
to the allure of divine perfection brings a transformative dynamic
into all material reality, namely, out of suffering into flourishing.
The work of practical reason is *to move* toward the good and out
of harm's way, *not to deliberate* cognitive metaphysical premises.
Thus understood, practical reason is a unique sort of "reflection on
praxis that illumines praxis," i.e., a unique rationality that is ordered
towards movement, not cognition.[25] Rhonheimer writes, "We are
concerned here not with a deductive, but rather a reflective process,
a constantly deepening reflection by the practical reason on one's
own action and judgment which—to employ an image—operates
not so much in a linear deductive, as in a circular or spiralling
inventive way.[26] Practical reason takes its point of departure from
the sensory experiences of harm and wellness, not from theoretical
judgements. The sensory corporeality knows when it is hurting and
when it feels well, knows progressive annihilation from flourishing,
knows the threat of death from the promise of life; the body knows
all these things without the speculations of intellectual nature. The
view from below sees apprehension as an experiential process. A
cumulative awareness, aggregating from lived experience, becomes
a practical know-how that Thomas has called reason. This rationality innate to the living body is clearly quite distinct from an intelligence of universals and speculation.

An innate way of knowing good from evil is a presumption
of Thomas's natural law; he has called this knowing, synderesis. He
refers to synderesis as a habit; in other words, it gets better with
practice. He links this habit of synderesis with practical reason:

> A man's act of reasoning, since it is a kind of movement,
> proceeds from the understanding of certain things—
> namely, those which are naturally known without in-
> vestigation on the part of reason, as from an immovable

24. Rhonheimer, "Practical Reason and the Naturally Rational," 106.
25. Rhonheimer, "Practical Reason and the Naturally Rational," 111.
26. Rhonheimer, "Practical Reason and the Naturally Rational," 120.

principle—and ends also at the understanding, inasmuch as it is by means of those principles naturally known, we judge of those things which we have discovered by reasoning. Now as it is clear that speculative reason argues about speculative things, so that practical reason argues about practical things. Therefore we must have, bestowed on us by nature, not only speculative principles but also practical principles. Now the first practical principles bestowed on us by nature, do not belong to a special power, but to a special natural habit, which we call synderesis.[27]

Synderesis has usually been considered a habit of the intellectual nature, which is the unfortunate consequence of viewing things exclusively from above. For example, Michael Sherwin has understood the principles of practical reason as universals, which position it as a capacity of the theoretical, speculative intellect. Citing Aquinas in *de veritatie,* Sherwin writes, "Judgement is twofold: about universals, and this pertains to synderesis, and about particulars, which belongs to the judgement of choice . . . (*liberem arbitrium*)."[28] Synderesis is indeed a principle, but perhaps more in the sense of a capacity for movement as opposed to a capacity for cognition. But as previously indicated, Rhonheimer makes clear the distinction between principle as a universal statement of the true and principle as impelling movement towards a particular, attractive good. Viewed from above, the conceptual truths and the good acts appear to be the same, but from below, the focus becomes the movement of advance from the false good towards the true good. Thus, oneness of the cognates, true and good, when viewed at the experiential level, take a life time of integration. From below, synderesis involves a life-long habit of scrutinizing the experiences of hurt, disappointment, betrayal, and loss, as well as love, joy, vitality, transformation, etc. so that the nature of the *true* good progressively takes on better clarity. Synderesis seen from below is a practice in which sensory nature becomes attuned (configured, inclined, intended, and so on) to one's innate sensory aptitude for knowing harm from good. On this view, synderesis is a practice, a habit, or a stance of sensory

27. ST I.79.12.

28. Sherwin, *By Knowledge and By Love,* 35, citing *De veritate* 24.1–17.

nature, which contributes to the know-how of practical reason, rather than to the syllogisms of theoretical reason. The view from below sees the human body becoming increasingly free for participating divine being (*capax dei*). It is only in participating the divine being that truth and goodness ultimately become the human experience of perfection, which ultimately becomes immune to the allures of mendacity.[29]

Numbed out from daily experiences of overwhelming violence, Martel's slave was doing what practical, lived experience had taught him to do, namely, to kill. By contrast, my patient, re-awakening to her difficult memories, was experiencing her passions anew—anger, fear, hope, and courage. The newly aroused passions restored to her a peculiar aspect of agency whereby she was subverting the bondage, the silencing, and the immobilization in which she had previously been existing. She too had been a slave of sorts, but, unlike the African slave, she was experiencing a powerful practical rationality that was moving her to become a different sort of person, namely, a free agent of her destiny, emerging progressively from the old victim identity. By contrast, Martel's brutalized, murderous slave was reduced to a practical reason impelling movements of bestial brutality. Both the African salve and the indigenous woman suffered the unspeakable, becoming mute victims paralyzed by overwhelming, annihilating circumstances. Their behavior was shaped not by speculative truths, but by the particular evils that had permeated and rendered infirm the deepest part of the self. The importance of the view from below is that it makes intelligible an approach based upon movement towards the possibility of human freedom for eternal wellbeing, a freedom that arises paradoxically and unpredictably out of the human experience of annihilation-as-destiny.

In modernity, we tend to default to the view from above; adopting the role of the helping observer, we are moved intellectually by the perceived moral imperative to offer speculative solutions for another's predicament. By contrast, the view from below engages practical reason, and lends validity and intelligibility to

29. For a more fulsome development of the resurrection of the body relevant to a sufferer's experience, see chapter 4.

the experience of suffering both directly and vicariously. Vicarious suffering might be parsed out as the experience of undergoing the felt *passions with* the sufferer who is telling—in other words, the experience of com-passion. On this view, vicarious suffering and compassion are experiences imprinted upon and located within sensory nature, experiences which I have *not* reduced to the cognates of problem-solving. The view from below legitimates refusal of the perspective that views suffering exclusively as a problem awaiting effective intervention. It is the sensed bodily feelings themselves (not emotions, not cognitions) that give rise to vicarious suffering—com-passion—in the attending professional. When sensory nature is thus understood as having its own rationality, one that is linked to the practical reason of (higher) intellectual nature, we have an important way of proceeding and attending the sufferer when analytical problem-solving is no longer called for.

SUMMARY

In this first chapter, I have firstly provided a concise version of Thomas on the sensory human nature. Human beings are possessed of a corporeality that moves according to a certain innate rationality towards flourishing. The primal intelligence wants to emerge from suffering, hurt, and harm—in short, it wants to emerge from the bondage of evil. The corporeality of which we are possessed is defined by its movements; when dead, the body becomes a decomposing corpse, no longer possessed of a desire by which it moves. In the second place, I have described suffering in terms of the hindrance or annihilation of this movement of advance towards flourishing. To describe such hindrance is to avoid glossing over the very real human experience of evil. In the third place, I focus upon the practical reason. Thomas has identified the rationality of particular acts (i.e., moves) as practical reason; I have recognized a link between this practical intelligence and the sensory nature, both of which Thomas describes as in pursuit of the good (flourishing), emerging from the bondage of evil (suffering).

It is important to note a certain contrast with the prevailing cultural paradigm. Our culture runs on science, which means that the tacit imperative is to restore the norm in the face of illness, i.e., when there is deviance from the norm. This prevailing paradigm is seen to be insufficient when we consider the suffering that persists in the face of effective technology and the competent restoration of empirically derived norms. Or in ethics, we have the persistence of suffering despite observance of and belief in the universal moral principles. The complementary paradigm that I am proposing on the basis of Thomas's understanding of human nature considers the gradient of movement from suffering towards flourishing. In order to appreciate this gradient, the perspective shifts to the view from below, where cognition is understood to be a secondary overlay.

In chapter 2, I explore in more detail this movement along the gradient from suffering to flourishing.

2

Movement in Thomas Aquinas

A Foundational Paradigm for Practical Ethics

The care-giving professional is often entrusted with someone's personal narrative of suffering. The theology that I am introducing arises from holding in my interiority many such narratives. I have asked, How am I to make sense of so much suffering and so many inconsolable sufferers? Although theology from a doctrinal perspective has not proven to be the best starting point for a professional life focused upon attending the sufferer, Thomas Aquinas on the dual capacities of human nature, namely, cognition and movement, offers potential for a theology of attending the sufferer. In this context, I am drawn to an exploration of movement, not cognitively derived therapy.

The first professional encounter with a sufferer is usually the "intake history" or "medical history." The analytic intellect listens poised to diagnose what has gone wrong and where there has arisen a deviance from the accepted norms. This effective approach is well-laid out in the professional standards of practice for the various disciplines. But listening for clues to suffering is less well specified and too often left to a sense of intuition that may (or may not) have undergone an ordered process of formation. Our default approach regards the facts of the matter at hand as variables in an equation, and the imperative at an ethical level is to offer a solution to the suffering. In other words, we assume that if we can identify and remedy the causes, the suffering will be resolved. But experience teaches us that most suffering does not go away through interventions based on the cause-effect paradigm.

The as yet unexplored heuristic is movement. I propose to research movement through the lens of philosophical and theological scholarship. Scholarship in ethics in the late twentieth century has recognized the risk of escalating suffering when moral agency is driven exclusively by the threat of penalty for failure to conform with obligatory external laws. I will propose that a more nuanced and robust understanding of moral agency lies in the exploration of the *act*, not as an external scrutiny of the objective righteousness of the act, but as an exploration of the human sufferer's interiority of apprehensive and appetitive movements proximal to an external manifestation of the act. The sufferer experiences—on the inside—that which both amplifies and hinders the vital and life-giving movements in pursuit of wellness. This is because the advance towards wellness and flourishing occurs in the context of the travail of emerging out of the silences and paralyses that have been imprinted by experiences of harm. The ever-intensifying dynamic of desire to flourish drives the act (movement) of advance. On this view, the default paradigm of penalty for transgression against external measures of righteousness, i.e., the imposition of measures intended to silence and to immobilize, is experienced as a silencing and immobilization of moral agency, which is the very meaning of suffering.[1]

I will contrast suffering-as-experience and suffering-as-cognate, arguing that when suffering is allowed to remain an experience of one's corporeality rather than abstracted from the narrative as a cognate for intellectual analysis, then there is potential for the sufferer to retrieve some degree of freedom from suffering, which is at the same time the freedom for movement towards wellbeing. This approach will enrich practice with theory by proposing a new heuristic in the face of moral tension; it will introduce a discourse,

1. See chapter 1.

which conveys the ethical potential of felt visceral movement. Complementary to the external nature of moral imperatives, the proposed ethics discourse will call forth a process of interior movement, placing value upon the felt visceral sense (the interiority) of the moral agent and the potential for an experience of transformation (movement) from suffering towards wellbeing. This emphasis involves an exploration of that which lies "deeper than" or "underneath" the emotions, affections, and cognitions generally associated with the human interiority.

HISTORICAL FOUNDATIONS

In her landmark paper of 1958, Modern Moral Philosophy, G. E. M. Anscombe questioned the prevailing understanding of ethics as tied to obligation.[2] Ethics as a system of laws and obligations implies adjudication, which reduces moral agency to the endurance of painful penalties. In other words, the empowered adjudicator may simply amplify the suffering when the perspective of the sufferer is suppressed. Anscombe was calling for a more nuanced ethics.

In pursuit of such nuance, in 1965, Germain Grisez turned to Thomas Aquinas on practical reason, i.e., the natural law.[3] He remarked on the slight mistranslation of Thomas's maxim describing practical reason: an imperative, "Do good and avoid evil." In this formulation, the role of practical reason was to discover a pre-existing good, with the obligation to do it, and to avoid what distracts from it. When Thomas's text was read differently, "Good is to be done and evil is to be avoided,"[4] then the imperative tone changed to a source of action. Action infers movement. Action, i.e., movement, is guided by the know-how aggregated through experience, not analysis. This rationality of action, described under his *questio* (or discussion) on Natural Law, was called practical reason by Thomas Aquinas. This kind of rationality did not follow the logic

2. Anscombe, *Modern Moral Philosophy.*

3. Grisez, "First Principle of Practical Reason."

4. "Bonum est faciendum et prosequendum, et malum vitandum" (ST I-II.94.2).

of imperatives but was rather a visceral tending towards the good, a disposition vulnerable to the hindrance of evil. Grisez brought to attention the potential of natural law as an approach to ethics more nuanced than obligation.

In 1993, in his encyclical *veritatis splendor*, Pope John Paul II began by emphasizing the human being's innate capacity to intellectually grasp the truth; one was both called to the truth (1 Pet 1:22) and yet susceptible to idols (Rom 1:25).[5] In modernity, the truth was confounded by "numerous doubts and objections of a human and psychological, social and cultural, religious and even properly theological nature."[6] The floundering intellect of analytical objectivity required a complementary guiding capacity. JPII called for a shift away from fear-filled imperatives and penalties towards a comportment impelled by love. "The commandment 'You shall not murder' becomes a call to an attentive love which protects and promotes the life of one's neighbor."[7] To live by love was to imitate the life of Christ, summarized in the scriptural beatitudes.[8] These habits of beatitude amounted to a choice for the vital dynamism of transformation and growth, precisely in life-draining circumstances. JPII brought much-needed attention to the human interiority, with its innate capacities for the true. But the distinction between the good and the true in the moral life would await future clarification.

In more contemporary times (2008) Martin Rhonheimer has turned the moral focus towards suffering; he points to a gap between "the [recognized] good and practicability."[9] A consequentialist ethics (such as Anscombe critiqued) evaluates the external act according to an *a priori* norm, and using logical argument, attempts to fill the gap between the theoretical good and the practical best-possible. But for Rhonheimer, this gap is human experience, "constituted by experiences of suffering injustice, disease, division

---

5. John Paul II, *Veritatis Splendor* 1.

6. John Paul II, *Veritatis Splendor* 4.

7. John Paul II, *Veritatis Splendor* 15.

8. John Paul II, *Veritatis Splendor* 16.

9. Rhonheimer, "Is Christian Morality Reasonable?," 8.

between men, unfaithfulness, war and violence, being powerless in the face of evil and of material and spiritual misery, and also our own weaknesses."[10] In this text, he retains suffering as human experience and does not revert to the language of abstract cognates falling under the scrutiny of moral norms. When suffering is reduced to *a cognate* (the view from above), ethics discourse arrives at logically defensible propositions predicting penalty, annihilation, and destruction. But when suffering retains *the experience* of the sufferer (the view from below), then practical reason and the felt sense of one's passions engage, impelling personal moral agency from suffering towards a state of flourishing previously unanticipated.

Thus, we have Anscombe's call to move away from an ethics of obligation, followed by Grisez's sense of progression by small practical steps towards an ultimate good, JPII's emphasis upon the interiority of the moral agent, and most recently, Rhonheimer's turn to one's personal, practical know-how in the context of felt experiences of suffering. The integrating common denominator of all these insights may be understood in terms of the observation of Thomas Aquinas, "Now life is shown principally by two actions, cognition and movement."[11] If cognition means concern with the true-in-general, then one aspect of cognition is the codification of truths into societal laws, which then obligate subordination for the sake of the common good. And so, it is an exercise of the cognition capacity that has given us our default heuristic, an ethics of obligation. Cognition has received much scholarly consideration, giving rise to the standard approach, i.e., "from above." But movement and its possible importance in the arena of both theory and practice as yet remains to be specified. The short historical progression outlined above invites the creative proposal of a new paradigm, one that is founded upon movement arising from and within the sensory nature rather than cognition of the intellectual nature.

To describe an experience of movement, without reducing it to a set of cognates, is to describe the dynamism of our very vitality and animation. This corporeal alive-ness breathes the air, pumps the

---

10. Rhonheimer, "Is Christian Morality Reasonable?," 8.
11. ST I.75.1.

blood, gesticulates, and makes facial expressions. It jumps and runs, it dances and swims, it gets tired, and it needs to rest. It also gets sick and hurt and sad, vulnerable to the intrusion of disease, to the injury of violence, and to the withdrawal of love. The experiences of our living moving sensory nature lend themselves to symbolism, which is not the same as analysis. In Genesis, the very experience of being alive is given a *symbolic* representation: movement in its primal form—the inspiration of breath—is like participating divine breathing. To be inspired and to breathe with the divine, is to evolve from being inert clay into a living human creature. The immobility of suffering, like inert clay inspired with the divine breath, evolves towards dynamic vitality and wellbeing, and ultimately towards an eternal cosmic dance that can suffer no restraints. Human sensory movement, at a symbolic level, is this advancing towards the good and out of harm's way. This felt sensing of movement aggregates into the perspective "from below," a paradigm of movement, that highlights inspiration not obligation, the giving of life not its depletion, and eternal animation not annihilation. A paradigm of movement enables the alluring experiences of life to trigger one's concupiscible appetite for eternal flourishing. On this view, eternal punitive predation upon one's well-being becomes an anxious, cognitive patterning arising from our fallen state.

AN ASPECT OF THE NEW PARADIGM: DISTINGUISHING BETWEEN THE GOOD AND THE TRUE

When the view is "from below," and the emphasis is upon the sensory domain of experience, it would seem important to maintain the distinction between the good and the true. Human beings often pursue what seems to be good and end up experiencing hurt because the alluring object proved to be a false good. Knowing what is true in general does not necessarily prevent such hurtful mistakes. Aware of this human vulnerability, Thomas Aquinas noted that we are not always able to move towards the good "on account of an impediment."[12] A human being, hindered by previous lived experiences, can confuse the good with the not-good, despite knowing full well what is true in general. Thomas made the important distinction between knowing intellectually what is true-in-general and knowing experientially what is good in a particular circumstance.[13] On this view, practical reason is the intelligence that works with the sensory nature in its movements towards the good of self-preservation, "warding off obstacles" and overcoming "impediments" to flourishing. To engage practical reason, we must suspend the ideas and propositions of our analytical, intellectual disciplines; practical reason arises from the sensory nature and its movements of attraction and aversion. To engage practical reason, we must approach from below and develop a sensed awareness of the movements of our corporeal sensory nature; the cognition/ thinking capacity of intellectual nature is not the exclusive common denominator of the human interiority. In knowing harm as misery and good as flourishing, the sensory nature furnishes a distinct rationality to human nature, which Thomas called the natural law. In colloquial terms, we might speak of the "gut sense." When we suspend the cognizing of natural law as moral obligation, i.e., suspend the view from above, it is this intelligent *movement*—both irascible and concupiscible—that comes into focus.[14] Practical reason then becomes that capacity of the intellectual nature that harnesses the sensed movement and felt vitality of our corporeality towards the moral pursuit of good and avoidance of evil. But practical reason works not through analytical speculation seeking the true-in-general but through the virtue/habit of prudence aggregated through the experiential felt-sensing of good as the converse of harm.

Although naturally impelled towards the good, the sensory nature often stumbles over goods that are not truly good. In other words, although the sensory nature tends naturally towards the good, it does not have the same propensity for the true. Anscombe describes the good as a matter of longing or appetite and the true

12. ST I-II.94.1.3.
13. ST I-II.94.2.
14. ST I-II.94.2.2.

as a matter of speculation or logic.[15] Whereas to pursue the true is to engage judgment and syllogistic progression, to sense movement toward the good is to feel desires and longings, attractions and aversions, and the hurt or misery that impedes flourishing. Thomas envisioned the interiority of the sensory nature as the locus of these movements, which he classified as sensory apprehensions and appetitions. When Thomas's elaboration of the sensory nature becomes the lens for the view "from below," we are able to understand good and evil in terms of particular experiences of flourishing and suffering. Rather than speak about good and evil in terms of universal cognates of right and wrong, our discourse turns to particular felt experiences of wellness and hurt.

To understand the perspective from below it is important to read Thomas on the sensory nature; his is a model of felt sensing that affords a perspective of the human interiority not captured by the empirical sciences such as a neurophysiology of sensation or a psychology of emotions. He describes a sensory interiority of apprehensive and appetitive capacities. The apprehensive part is complex.[16] The familiar five senses interact with the exterior milieu, and a complex system of interior senses interprets the lived experiences as harmful or useful towards flourishing. This interpretation by felt sense happens at the level of the corporeal physicality, a level which is not to be conflated with the practical reason of our higher intellectual nature. The internal sense of memory is comprised of sensory imprints (phantasms) of lived experiences, which are collated by the cogitative sense into a kind of primal knowing about harm/hurt/evil and wellness/pleasure/good. The primal knowing of the sensory nature is concealed within the interiority and is not accessible to the empirical observer. This knowing configuration of the interiority is referred to as intention, described by Anscombe as that which is known without observation, e.g., the position of one's limbs.[17] We know many such things by the felt sense of our corporeality, the intellectual cogitation at that moment a dormant overlay.

15. Anscombe, *Intention*, 13.

16. ST I.75–89. See also part II of Pasnau, *Thomas Aquinas on Human Nature*.

17. Anscombe, *Intention*, 13.

This concealed sensory interiority of *intentiones* becomes the configuration from which appetitive movement arises. Because the imprinted *intentiones* have integral meanings of harm and good, the related appetitive movement plays out as a tending towards the good out of harm's way. For Thomas, the appetitive movements of sensory nature are the passions, movements of our corporeality, or "transmutations" in response to experiences of good or evil.[18] These transmutations happen at a primal level independently of the higher intellect. (Although the mind may trigger passions, it is not the necessary pre-requisite for a passion to arise.) In contrast to contemporary models, Thomas did not view the concealed sensory interiority in terms of the workings of hidden thoughts and cognitions; the sensory nature had its own primal "smarts" from whence it mounted a response to experiences of hurt and wellbeing. Which is not to say that the intellect cannot modulate responsiveness. But the view from below understands this modulation as a layer superimposed upon the primal event of corporeal transmutation in response to external events. Because Thomas maintains a distinction between the "higher" intellectual nature and the "lower" sensory nature, one can justify proceeding according to a view "from above" or "from below." The hidden human interiority does not boil down to cognition alone; the felt apprehensions and appetitions of the sensing corporeality are an integral and perhaps an overlooked aspect of the human interiority.

In order to illustrate how the view from above with its intellectual speculations of cognition overlooks the sensory nature and its movement, I will summarize the work of Daniel DeHaan on the cogitative sense. He subdivides sensory apprehension into the capacities to sense and to perceive. The presence or absence of an object, and its colour, number, shape, texture, temperature, etc. are sensibles. Using the essential sensibles of a duck or a rabbit, one can then perceive the ambiguity of a puzzle that may look like a duck or a rabbit at the same time. Or the sensibles of gold and mountain may come together in the perception of a golden mountain. This type of perception is referred to by Thomas as the

18. ST I-II.22.

forming of *intentiones,* or what I would call imprints with intrinsic meanings. DeHaan coins the term "percept" to elaborate more precisely the *intentio* formed by the cogitative power of the sensory nature.[19] Interpreting Thomas from above, in terms of cognition (not movement), he writes, "These. . . intentions specify a formal object that belongs to the spectrum of cognitive operations that Aquinas used to differentiate an internal sense power called "natural instinct' or the 'estimative power' in nonhuman animals, and the 'cogitative power,' 'particular reason,' and the 'passive intellect" in human beings."[20] On this view, the particular reason/cogitative sense is less an aspect of the "smart" sensory corporeality, and more a cognition of the intellectual nature, albeit inextricably linked with sensory appetition. Engaging his own speculative rationality, DeHaan classifies the cogitative sense as having aspectual, actional, and affectional "percepts." Having classified sensory apprehension in terms of cognition, DeHaan's model overlooks the experiential know-how that wants to avoid hurt and advance—move—towards felt sensory well-being.

In order to illumine the contrasting view from below, I will turn the above perspective upside down. I will describe the cogitative sense/particular reason in terms of *a particular felt experience of movement* and not as a kind of cognition. An example will serve to allow an image of rational or "smart" movement to emerge. A pianist learns a piece by analyzing the chordal structures and the modulations through various keys. At first he plays the piece of music informed by this work of the analytical mind, but eventually the notes are in the body memory. When the notes are in the body memory, he no longer thinks analytically as he plays; he is now able to express through the movement of his fingers the movements of his passions. Music-making is movement that communicates; such communication depends upon the sensory nature with its appetitive vitality. Therein lies the remarkable intelligence of the movement. It is not simply an analysis of the score, which would

19. In Thomas, there are many other usages of the term *intentio* which do not refer to the sensory nature (see DeHaan, "Perception and the *Vis Cogitativa,*" 409).

20. DeHaan, "Perception and the *Vis Cogitativa,*" 397–437.

require nothing beyond the speculative theoretical intelligence. Music-making requires the sensory nature with its specific kind of intelligence around movement. When the pianist slips during a performance and plays a "wrong note," the cogitative sense immediately recognizes that sound as a slip, even before the intellectual nature engages. The experienced pianist is not put off despite the slip and continues his performance as a musical communication.

Keeping the example of the pianist in mind, we will now regard the moral act through the same lens of movement. The moral act may also be seen as a movement of communication; it expresses imprinted experiences of harm and of good, i.e., it is a communication that arises, like music-making, from the depth of the sensory interiority. The moral imperatives and prohibitions are the elements that may be analyzed, like the chordal structures of the piece of music to be learned. But these theoretical principles or generalities are insufficient to choreograph the moral movement/act in the particular circumstances at hand. The moral act, when the sensory nature is fully alive, becomes a unique communication of the personal interiority of imprinted experiences and arising passions in pursuit of flourishing and avoidance of harm. But such moral movement is not stereotypical or normative; it is particular to the agent's abilities and expressive of the agent's past. Imprints of harm give rise to certain kinds of reactive passions, i.e., under the *intentio* of imprints of harm, the moral act may take on an appearance that is incoherent with the imperative issued by an observer. This is not to say that moral absolutes are irrelevant; it is to allow for the internalization of such imperatives, a process that necessarily involves the subjective agency of integrating moral absolutes with personal imprints of harm and wellbeing. This process of agency is concealed from the observer and belongs exclusively to the sufferer-as-moral-agent. On this view, agency means that the sensory interiority undergoes shifts in identity as the imprints of harm and of flourishing undergo the arduous process of transformation and arrive ultimately to a state of beatific flourishing and no more suffering.

This emphasis upon one's vulnerability to evil, the healing from imprints of harm, and the pursuit of flourishing stands in stark contrast to a morality that works with adjudication, culpability, and penalty. In a context of healing from harm in pursuit of flourishing, an adjudicated infliction of suffering becomes a less persuasive approach to becoming good. Thus, when we retain the distinction between the good and the true, afforded by the view from below, we see a vulnerable seeker advancing little by little towards the good, and we avoid imposing penalties that would only hinder by more suffering her attainment of the good.

THINKING IN THE NEW PARADIGM: *TWO DISTINCT METANARRATIVES*

Having identified my rootedness within the theological/philosophical tradition, and having illustrated the contrast between the true and the good, I shall now propose two complementary metanarratives to guide our ethics discourse, one in pursuit of the true and the other as a felt advance towards some viscerally sensed good. The former works with a paradigm of cognition and the latter with a paradigm of movement. While narrative is currently viewed as having the potential to point our ethics discourse beyond the impersonal imperatives of principlism, the rigor and structure of such narrative inquiry remain to be specified. It is this project of specification that I now address. My interlocutors for this section—Alasdair MacIntyre, Servais-Théodore Pinckaers, David Burrell, and Rita Charon—cross the boundaries between theology, philosophy, and medical practice.

Alasdair MacIntyre addresses the central question in ethics in *Ethics and the Conflicts of Modernity*: "What should I do?" He adds, "What is it that I want?" And then more precisely, "Do I have sufficiently good reasons to want what I now want . . . [and to act as I am acting?]."[21] For MacIntyre, ethics is a process of reasoning; one must have "good reasons." Good desiring, wanting, and longing evidently come subsequently. Acts become intelligible if one's desires are rationally ordered towards the good.[22] On this view, objectivity as well as external valuing are important factors in

21. MacIntyre, *After Virtue*, 4–8.
22. MacIntyre, *After Virtue*, 9.

moral agency, particularly when the concern is to refute emotivist/ expressivist accounts of the good, as MacIntyre is doing. Expressivism is characterized by moral statements, which express not only beliefs but also attitudes of approval and disapproval. Thus, in the expressivist paradigm, the underlying psychology of the teller and the listener play a role in determining the moral good. This sets up "an opposition between reason and passion, or reason and desire."[23] Yet, the expressivists do have a point in that desire *is* necessary for action; facts, including statements of reasonableness, do not move us to action unless coupled with desire. MacIntyre addresses this objection by inserting flourishing as a synonym for the good; legitimate desire seeks the good. The problematic issue for MacIntyre is the emotional relativism, whereby what feels good must indeed be good. He takes a reactive opposite stance: the good must measure up against the true-in-general.[24] Thus human flourishing as a good is no longer an experience but rather becomes a cognate that serves as a reference point in choosing what is to be done. In like manner, desire-as-experience must undergo the test of reasonableness, and so desire either meets the benchmark of reason or fails to measure up. On this view, the conflict between desire and reason is incontestable. This is the premise from which MacIntyre builds his argument. He refers to the conflict between what one desires and what one rationally ought to desire as "a lacuna" that calls for a "much richer understanding of the psychology of morality" than has previously been elucidated.[25] However, if one were to explore flourishing as a felt experience of the sensory corporeal nature, then our understanding of morality would evolve beyond the restrictions of a normative ethics informed by sciences such as psychology.

MacIntyre is, of course, a respected scholar from a tradition that adheres to the perspective from above, by which I mean that he appeals to a logical flow grounded in a science such as psychology, to normative standards of the true-in-general, to the logical conflict between reason and desire, and to cognates rather than

23. MacIntyre, *After Virtue,* 21.

24. MacIntyre, *Ethics,* 25.

25. MacIntyre, *Ethics,* 33.

experiences. This perspective leads him to a pattern of moral reasoning that proceeds according to what I will call a metanarrative of the true-in-general. It has become our default stance in ethics discourse. I will argue that this metanarrative of the true-in-general is insufficient when the ethical question arises, What am I *to do*? Or How am I *to move* forward? The metanarrative of the true awaits the specification of a complementary metanarrative that calls forth the dynamic know-how of our sensing-desiring physicality complete with its movements of vitality.

If MacIntyre has contrasted reason and desire, Servais-Théodore Pinckaers has articulated a contrast between distinct rationalities. The "logic" of the Holy Spirit is not the same as the reason of Cartesian or Kantian or even Scholastic logic.[26] Paranesis—morality by imperative—is a product of modern philosophical/theological thought, shaped by the tradition of the Moral Manuals in which the Decalogue is appropriated as a juridical template. By contrast, the logic of the Spirit is apprehended through paraclesis—exhortation—as in the letters of St. Paul or in the Sermon on the Mount. The ancient tradition, from which Jesus came, privileged wisdom over propositional logic, in which the state of flourishing came about as movement through and beyond a state of suffering or misery (Matt 5:3–4, 9–11). In Scripture, misery is not a cognate; it is specified as particular experiences. Poverty, loss, discord, violence, animosity, victimization, or in other words human misery, are framed as the *experiential* matrix from which flourishing may arise according to the mysterious, creative dynamism of the Spirit of God. The Beatitudes call us forth to transformation[27] at the level of the sensory interiority in response to felt suffering. This statement is true-in-general; it is a given. The moral life does not involve arguing this truth in the abstract. What the moral life does involve is the progressive freedom to undergo experientially the movement of shifting from misery into beatitude, and perhaps to accompany others immersed in the same process. The experience of

26. Pinckaers, "Scripture and the Renewal of Moral Theology."
27. Burrell, *Learning to Trust in Freedom*, 45.

participation in the dynamic of such transformation from suffering to flourishing is one aspect of the metanarrative of becoming well.

David Burrell's work adds to my proposed metanarrative of becoming well. He has described wellness in terms of becoming free from the imperatives of our pre-conceived but limiting idea of the moral good so that one might become free for a creative responsiveness to the dynamism and contingencies of life. Burrell contrasts "the free dynamic of invitation and response" with an unnecessary discourse of explanation.[28] When we let go of the compulsion for logical explanations, we have a paradigm in which we are free to be "compelled by the lives, [of saintly exemplars of goodness], inspired and illuminated by [their] narratives." When explanations are de-emphasized, doctrine becomes a secondary grammatical tool for speaking about the general elements common to inspiration, illumination, and transformation. In contrast to the ideology of doctrine, transformation-as-experience feels like an invitation to participate in the life of the one whose narrative inspires. This is not the free-form feeling-domain of expressivism. Nor is it the analytical, objectifying gaze of the dispassionate observer—clinician, moralist, or judge. This is the domain of the sufferer, who in the voice of the first person speaks a "fine grained" narrative of particularities, subjectivities, and contingencies. The narrative of the one who is experiencing full-bodied personal feelings runs unexpectedly counter to modernity's generalizations around the empirically proven inevitability of destruction.[29] When experience is allowed to displace explanation there arises a kind of freedom. It is freedom from preconceived ideas—cognitions—that have delimited and immobilized. And it is a freedom for participation in a process of becoming re-animated. Such freedoms are experienced at the level of the passions of the visceral sensory nature. When feeling-experiences are viewed as passions, the intellectual need for psychological explanations and analytical justifications is defused. The passions of the sensory nature are in accord with a rationality that refuses the compulsion of our culture for explanation; the

---

28. Burrell, *Learning to Trust in Freedom*, 49.
29. Burrell, *Learning to Trust in Freedom*, 61.

sensory nature awakens a rationality that is content to abide in the movements of concupiscence and irascibility aroused by experiences of freedom. A metanarrative of becoming well exposes the passions—visceral feeling-experiences—of a sensory nature that bends and inclines itself out of harm's way towards the good, i.e., towards a felt sense of wellbeing.

The relevance of these two distinct metanarratives for the analytical thinker is brought into the clinical arena by Rita Charon, an internist who initiated the narrative medicine movement. Without diminishing the importance of diagnostic analytics, narrative medicine highlights the importance of allowing one's subjective visceral resonance to engage when listening to the patient narrative. While the analytic modality of listening for symptoms of disease is essential to diagnostic acuity, the capacity to resonate with the sufferer is an equally important aptitude. There is a physicality involved in this deep listening.[30] For Charon, the physicality of listening gives rise to desire, echoing the Thomistic model in which apprehension gives rise to desire and appetitive movement. When the dynamism of visceral sense and physical desire are engaged, the potential for movements of transformation can be seen. The story being told can shift, like a dream shifts and changes, bringing about a parallel transformation in the teller. Laurie Zoloth, an ethicist in the narrative medicine movement, considers this ontologic potential of narrative to be the essence of ethics.[31] The listening, the conversation, and the relationship between the teller and the listener engage each person in a full-bodied manner (without suppressing the analytical capabilities) giving rise to ontologic transformation. What Zoloth is doing is taking the view from below, from which perspective she can see this dynamic of the sensory nature fully alive impelled towards transformative shifts in identity. This physical dynamism of the sensibilities and desires—movement—is a defining aspect of the proposed metanarrative of becoming well.

---

30. Charon, *Narrative Medicine*, 124–25.

31. Charon and Zoloth, "Like an Open Book," 28.

APPLYING THE NEW PARADIGM:
FROM THEORY TO PRACTICE

When immersed in the moral tension of what might be good to do for now under the circumstances, we may resist the prevailing habit of lining up moral principles in the interest of explanations and problem-solving. We now have an alternative approach that involves listening for occasions of suffering and attending to the felt sense of knowing that resonates within our personal visceral space. The questions guiding our deliberations then become, Who is the sufferer? How might I describe his "stuckness?" How is she, the next-of-kin, exhibiting movement? Is something actively hindering the feeling of wellness? How might I articulate this particular person's vulnerability to getting hurt? What would flourishing look like? What would annihilation look like. . . and animation? Is there a language of symbolism or metaphor in play around experiences of good and of evil? These are the questions unique to an ethics discourse stimulated by the proposed metanarrative of becoming well, which complements and contrasts with the prevailing imperative of getting things right. The underlying visceral knowing arises from the feeling-experience of movement towards and participation in an ineffable eternal becoming, which is supremely good. In Christian parlance, one speaks of a graced awareness that effectively subverts the argument that death offers the ultimate solution to suffering.

SUMMARY

In this chapter I have focused the reader's attention once again upon the vital sensory nature, with its unique and wondrous sensibilities and longings, having aggregated wisdom from experiences of both flourishing and suffering. This sensory nature has a vital role in our moral becoming, especially when oppressive circumstances bring about intellectual confusion around the universal moral principles. While intellectual confusion would tend to obfuscate moral clarity around the issue at hand, the sensory nature still remains ordered in a primal manner towards aliveness and wellness, away from annihilation and harm. Practical ethics, although necessarily informed by universal principles, need not begin with the speculative, theoretical goal of the right and true. On this alternate view (from below), the starting point is the sufferer's experience of immobilization and silencing, and the goal is one small practical step of advance out of this state of "stuckness" into a restored and intensified dynamic vitality that participates the sacred mystery of ultimate Being. Thomas Aquinas understands that ultimate Being to be pure *actus;* to participate the divine *actus* means that mundane human movements are elevated to potential moral agency.

In chapter 3, I will explore this participating the divine *actus* as the necessary incorporation of mystery into a culture whose greatest strength has been its capacity to de-mystify by a deployment of the scientific method. However, as stated earlier, suffering remains essentially a mystery that is not amenable to the empirical measurements and abstract mathematics of the scientific method. The sufferer calls forth in us a complementary heuristic.

3

The Ineffable in Clinical Discourse

In a culture such as ours, where the only belief system acceptable in a public forum is restricted to the cause-effect paradigm of science, one asks the question, Could there be relevant meaning in the ineffable? I will approach this question from the intersection of medicine-as-science, spirituality-as-mystery, and ethics as the interface between the two. I will take the position that suffering calls forth both a process of de-mystification (science) and the preservation of mystery (spirituality). The methodology of science is to problematize suffering as a matter to be mastered and solved. But experience teaches us that suffering has a way of persisting despite well-studied, evidence-based interventions. The response to this collective experience in the healthcare context has been the proliferation of such idioms as patient-centered care, narrative medicine, the medical humanities, and contemplative care. When a sufferer reveals a personal narrative of suffering it is not the same as the narrative constructed about that person (the object) by the observing professional (the subject). Attending the sufferer's experience rather than attending to the problem-solving calls for a methodology, indeed a new paradigm, that will complement the subject-object paradigm of our modern science-based cultures.

If not assessing a collection of symptoms and signs according to the universal evidence-based norms of physiology, psychology, or sociology, how is the listening clinician to approach the patient's narrative? In chapter 1, I suggested that the pre-modern dynamics of the sensory corporeality (as per Thomas Aquinas) could provide a logical but non-scientific basis for understanding the mystery of human experiencing. In the second chapter, I observed that most "intake histories" are narratives of suffering-as-experience and not suffering-as-problem awaiting professional intervention. In this third chapter, the analytic way of listening in order to problem-solve will be temporarily suspended in the interest of evolving a complementary paradigm that engages the listener's visceral sensibilities in response to suffering. In our technologically charged, statistically driven culture of interventional effectiveness and efficiency, it is the humanities that cultivate a nuanced—but un-measurable—responsiveness to suffering. But, if it is not the norms and universals, then what is it about the humanities that enable the helping professional to be truly present?

In offering an answer to this question, certain assumptions need to be identified. The terms suffering and flourishing will be juxtaposed. These terms will signify what is harmful and what is good for the particular person who is revealing a narrative of suffering. While harm and good have often been considered as abstract and universal principles of evil and righteousness, in this chapter, suffering and flourishing will be understood not as abstract cognates but rather as lived experiences of harm and good. When considered as personal experiences of suffering and flourishing, the subjective, physical reality of difficult circumstances comes into focus. This lived reality, viewed through the lens of one's primal physicality, amounts to a desire for and an advance towards wellbeing with an aversion to and an avoidance of annihilation. In contrast to a predictable certainty in the laws of nature, this experiential dynamic focuses one's attention upon contingency, ambivalence, and uncertainty. Each person's experience is uniquely and unaccountably their own, and not an exemplar of some generalization.

The dynamic of suffering-advancing-towards-flourishing includes the experience of something unexpectedly life-giving or good that penetrates such hurtful happenings of contingency as disease, war, or natural disaster. Therein lies the experience of the ineffable, the inexplicable, and the mysterious. This aspect of mystery in human existence is assumed in the theological literature. When the theological literature is introduced into healthcare and integrated with the medical humanities, a fresh paradigm begins to suggest itself. This fresh paradigm is well-suited to companioning the mysterious, transformative dynamic of advance from suffering towards flourishing. Beginning with my particular experience (as a healthcare professional), I grope towards an as yet inchoate universal of meaning that has the potential to undergird our attending and companioning the human sufferer.

By citing the theological literature, my intention is not to proselytize healthcare with abstract doctrines and religious ideologies, but rather to call us forward as care-givers, to new horizons and possibly a new world-view in which mystery *in and of itself* is important for the art of companioning the sufferer. While I have explored only one tradition, the Christian tradition, with a fresh in depth reading of Thomas Aquinas on human nature, others might want to explore different traditions for more insights into a responsiveness to suffering that comprises a common good. The paradigm that I am proposing is not intended to be comprehensive; I believe that there is an untapped potential for the pre-modern understanding of human nature to evolve into a new paradigm to guide the post-modern agent who encounters and becomes witness to a narrative of suffering.

In the first part of this chapter, some of the relevant scholarship in both the medical and in the theological literature around the mystery aspect of suffering/flourishing will be presented. In the second part, towards a clinical application of my research, two contrasting overarching narratives will be developed by means of two distinct expositions of a woman's moral conundrum around the abortion of her pregnancy. Finally, in concluding, I will propose that a robust clinical approach is informed not only by the metanarrative of scientific de-mystification but also by a complementary metanarrative around an essential, humane, felt sense of mystery in both the sufferer and the attending clinician. It is the specification of this metanarrative of mystery to which I now turn.

BACKGROUND SCHOLARSHIP:
SUFFERING AS MYSTERY

Anne Hudson Jones has suggested that, for the clinician, narratives of suffering have a certain primacy over medical science and moral principles.[1] While abstract ideas have driven the sciences to great discoveries and the resolution of disease states, there is also an undeniable intuition that the human experience of suffering accompanying disease is elusive and somehow ineffable.

Contrasting the mindset of science-based care with the ineffable element in contemplative care, Bradley Lewis has noted that the spiritual traditions regard suffering as senseless and yet find a way to make sense of it all.[2] To make sense of experiences that do not fit into the norms and principles of our contemporary, science-based culture is to inscribe that narrative of suffering into an overarching metanarrative. This rather countercultural response to suffering does not seek to correct, to erase, or to problem-solve suffering.

Elizabeth Lewis Hall, integrating theology and psychology, speaks to this cultural imperative of relieving the sufferer of the suffering. When the sufferer embraces such difficult feelings as aversion, anger, sadness, fear, and despondency, new insights about the circumstances and the self may arise. She regards as hedonistic a cultural approach that "sees pleasure as good and pain as bad," pointing to an ancient philosophical distinction between pleasure and flourishing. On this view, the good life as the exclusive pursuit of pleasure is regarded negatively as hedonism; by contrast, the good as a movement of advance from misery towards flourishing is understood as a mysterious healing transformation.[3]

---

1. Hudson Jones, "Literature and Medicine," 1243–46.

2. Lewis, "Narrative Medicine and Contemplative Care," 309–24.

3. Hall et al., "Role of Suffering in Human Flourishing," 111–21.

Where the goal is healing transformation, nothing needs to be resolved and no decisions need to be made, according to Arthur Frank. On this view, narrative offers a "medium of becoming." Story-telling takes on a moral dimension; one thinks with the story and allows it to lead to the next step.[4] Storied rationality is neither analytical (cause and effect) nor syllogistic (if this happens, then that must follow); artful narrative enables a rationality that is well-suited to the unique contingencies of a life lived. Storied thinking can afford a moral agent the freedom of doing the best possible thing for now under the circumstances. It is in sharp contrast to an ethics conceived speculatively according to abstract principles of the true-in-general, where, in place of freedom, the moral agent experiences the constraints of *a priori* norms. While the norms may well be true in general, a practical pursuit of healing transformation is to arrive in a storied advance at the freedom for becoming a more fully flourishing human being.

For David Burrell such freedom is not simply a freedom to follow the rules and to fit oneself into the predefined norms; human freedom involves participation in an ineffable creative process that overflows all rules and norms.[5] The capacity for such mysterious ontologic creativity is concealed within the human interiority and does not lend itself to the measures of laws of nature, psycho-social norms, and other external benchmarks. When the response to suffering is an ever-increasing desire to flourish rather than an obligatory imperative to erase the suffering, then the human interiority can begin to open up beyond the rule-bound modality of cause-effect explanations into "the free dynamic of invitation and response."[6] This responding to suffering with the primal but complex longing to flourish shapes one's becoming accordingly. The experience of flourishing reinforces the desire to flourish and activates the innate freedom for experiences of flourishing. This is where the imperative of the third person observer falls short. The imperative to problem-solve suffering by applying a cause-effect paradigm leads to

---

4. Frank, *Wounded Story-Teller*, 159–60.

5. Burrell, *Learning to Trust in Freedom*, xv.

6. Burrell, *Learning to Trust in Freedom*, 49.

empirical observations around never-ending cycles of violence and abstract conclusions around inevitable, eternal destruction. Such cause and effect thinking leads to a hopelessness that precludes wellbeing. Suffering understood as an abstraction in terms of cause, effect, and solution stands in sharp contrast to suffering regarded as an experience of longing for flourishing and release from harm. The former is the work of scientific de-mystification that inevitably concludes with the empirically obvious death-is-the-end; the latter is a narrative of ineffable small joys and experiences of flourishing in the very face of impending annihilation.

The Abrahamic spiritual traditions are inspired by narratives of companioning the sufferer who is hungry, destitute, sick, and lonely. This is in contrast to the unschooled human inclination to scapegoat and to ostracize such persons as a blight upon society, as elaborated in the work of René Girard.[7] Michael Dodds, a theologian in the Christian tradition, depicts the stance of companioning. On this view, the interiority of each person is imbued with a sacred Presence. It is a creative, life-giving Presence that identifies with and abides within the lived personal matrix of human suffering and flourishing.[8] To experience this abiding Presence is to experience also a kind of kindred spirit between self and other in the shared quest for advance out of harm's way towards flourishing. It is from this ineffable experience of the Sacred, infusing wellbeing in the face of hurt, that there arises the human capacity to reach out to the suffering other. On this view, the disengaged observer, speculating about suffering in terms of cause, effect, and solution, lacks the nuance of a full-bodied human presence. By contrast, a clinical listener, who experiences full-bodied, visceral resonance in response to a narrative of overwhelming hurt, companions and supports the ontological becoming of the teller. Such companioning, grounded in the ineffable, is well-suited to the goal of patient-centered care and a humane response to suffering.

7. Girard, *I See Satan Fall.*
8. Dodds, "Thomas Aquinas, Human Suffering," 330–44.

Lisa Rosenbaum reflects on the election of that which is life-giving in the face of overwhelming evil. She describes the murder of a colleague.

> Around 11:00 a.m. on Jan 20, 2015, Stephen Pasceri arrives at the cardiovascular cnter at Boston's Brigham and Women's Hospital, where he had an appointment to speak to Michael Davidson, a forty-four-year-old surgeon who had performed valve surgery on Pasceri's mother a few months earlier. Davidson entered an exam room and greeted Pasceri, who fired two shots at the surgeon at close range before killing himself. A team of surgeons spent nine hours in the OR in a futile attempt to save Davidson's life.[9]

In the wake of such violence, with all the fear and anger, how can one keep on going?

> Tragedy can have meaning without having reason, and that's as true for us as it is for our patients. To seek reasons for the tragic loss of Michael Davidson is to become afraid. To seek meaning is, in a sense, to do the opposite.[10]

She suggests that although the fear is real and powerful, it need not define one's comportment. Life and meaning—wellbeing—can be found within an extraordinary experience of harm and annihilation. But when the goal is to refuse to be manipulated by fear, evidence-based information and the workings of reason are not the required disposition. A deeper interiority is inferred in which meaning can offer something more compelling than reason.

For an understanding of these deep interior sensibilities, I turn to Thomas Aquinas, because his pre-modern interpretation of human corporeality is helpful in getting beyond the modern bias that efficiently restore science-based norms.[11] Aquinas understands human nature as not only an intelligence around universals but in the first place as the sensory body moving always out of the bondage of suffering towards a freedom for flourishing. Towards that

9. Rosenbaum, "Being Like Mike," 798–99.
10. Rosenbaum, "Being Like Mike," 799.
11. ST I.75–89; I-II.22–48.

end, the internal senses are designed to interpret lived experiences in terms of harmful (bad) or helpful (good) for flourishing. Another capacity of the internal senses is to store these experience-based meanings in the body memory. From these concealed imprints of lived experience arise the "appetites." The appetitive passions and desires move us and keep us going forward towards wellbeing even in the wake of petrifying, paralyzing violence. This model of human nature is not science-based, and yet it can explain the comportment of a physician such as Rosenbaum, who turns away from that which literally petrifies and paralyzes towards that which inspires hope and vitality. The fear, the anger, and the potential for vengeance is there, but the passion that prevails by choice is to attend the sufferer who struggles to advance towards flourishing. Here we consider not only the patient as sufferer, but also the sufferer concealed within the interiority of the clinician. In making this mysterious choice for sustaining and supporting life in the wake of paralyzing annihilation and terrifying destruction, Rosenbaum is effectively offering a metanarrative of meaning that inspires freedom for that which is life-giving. To be inspired with the freedom to undergo deep personal change is not the goal of reason and our modern sciences.

This brief summary of the overlapping areas of scholarship in the medical humanities and theology provides some themes of relevance to the practice of medicine.

1. A unique interiority within each human being yearns for flourishing but is hindered by difficult circumstances.
2. Companioning a sufferer involves a felt visceral resonance in response to the patient- narrative.
3. The visceral responsiveness matures into a storied longing for flourishing that knows when to suspend the problem-solving.
4. Interior freedom to companion the vulnerable sufferer towards flourishing is at the same time a freedom to refuse the prevailing assumption that evil/suffering ought to be rationally problem-solved.

These themes (and potentially many others) suggest a metanarrative for the new discourse in medicine around the primacy of narratives of suffering, the relevance of a spiritual practice, the narrative as the medium of one's ontological becoming, and a patient-centered approach that goes beyond offering options in treatments, styles, and personnel.

To facilitate the practice of a heightened clinical sensibility around suffering/flourishing, I will now develop two distinct yet complementary metanarratives. One will proceed according to the prevailing method of critical analysis in academic scholarship, a method which distinguishes itself by the capacity to problematize, to intervene, and to problem-solve. The other metanarrative will represent a proposed manner of proceeding when the goal is the mysterious medical art of attending the sufferer.

CASE PRESENTATION ACCORDING TO PREVAILING SCHOLARSHIP

The scenario is about one woman's struggle with the decision for abortion as presented in an article on informed consent by Diana Fritz Cates, a bioethicist with a scholarly interest in Thomas Aquinas.[12] The scene is a conversation between three girlfriends in their student days, Judy, Laura, and Diana (the author):

> Judy has decided to have an abortion because "When I told Don that I was pregnant, he got really quiet. I was hoping that he'd be happy . . . but he wasn't. . . . It took a couple of days, but I managed to get him to tell me what was wrong. He told me about his father—about the years of physical and emotional abuse. The idea of being a father himself fills him with terror. . . . He doesn't trust his instincts on this. He's not ready. . . . I'm afraid that if I were to go through with this pregnancy I would lose Don. . . . Our marriage would come undone and I'd be left to raise a kid on my own. . . . I can't handle it." [Judy's friend Laura responds], "But Judy, you told me a couple of months ago, after your dad died, that you wanted a baby more than anything else in the world. . . . And now you want to destroy it?"

12. Cates, "Caring for Girls and Women," 162–203.

[Diana Fritz Cates, the third friend in the trio and author of this citation, reflects on the conversation in hindsight]. "Don had so much influence over her choice. . . . It seemed strange to Laura that, although Judy was upset over how the conversation was going, she did not appear to be very upset at the prospect of the abortion itself." [Fritz Cates goes on to observe that where Judy did manifest emotion was around Don's well-being. The problem was not so much that Judy suffered when Don was suffering, but that Judy's] "co-suffering. . . seemed to be dominating [her] deliberations. . . . After receiving Don's reaction, [Judy had decided to] disengage emotionally from her fetus." [Fritz Cates continues], "I wondered whether it was a good idea for Judy to be making a decision of this magnitude in what appeared to be a state of selective emotional numbness." [Certain] "relevant information could be gleaned only by feeling (and at the same time reflecting upon) certain painful emotions."

CASE PRESENTATION AS TOLD BY THE SUFFERERS

Judy. I am pregnant, Don! It is the answer to a deep longing that has grown so intense in me as I have grieved by father's death. I feel such deep joy and peace as I let this new situation really sink in.

Don. I am frightened, Judy. My father was not a good model for me. He beat me and humiliated me endlessly. I still feel that I am not a whole person, not really ready to be a father.

Judy. Don, you are not your father. Nor are you your father's victim anymore. Now it is you and me and our baby. You are a kind and gentle husband, and there is no reason that you could not grow to become a good father. I know you have it in you because of how you are with me.

Don. I feel so paralyzed by my past, Judy, condemned to be the same ogre that my father was. You know, like the victim becomes the victimizer.

Judy. True enough, but it does not have to be that way. Yes, you may make mistakes along the way, but you can learn from the mistakes. I will be learning too. No one is exactly the book-perfect parent. Of course, we all strive for that but. . .

Don. Maybe I will arrange for some counselling, although that feels daunting too. Where to start? What will I say? But, in the end it might help me feel more courageous. Of course, I won't have progressed very far by the time the baby arrives. . . . You know, I think you should simply have an abortion, and we will try for another pregnancy when I am ready.

Judy. Hmmm. Your process around counselling will help you come to peace with the hurts of the past. But it won't make you a picture-perfect parent. That can only come from the experience of holding the baby, holding it when it cries, when it learns to laugh, when it learns to walk and talk, and holding it all the way into adulthood, and even then continuing to laugh and cry as we all journey through this life together.

Don. No Judy, I am not ready for fatherhood.

Judy. Get out of your head, Don. If I have an abortion, do you really think it will bring you healing from the violence of the past? Violence upon violence sounds to me like just a bigger pile of violence.

Don. Oh God. . . . How will I ever be rid of that terrible feeling of being unworthy of love and incapable of loving? I feel so stuck. . . . And yet, I do want to move on.

Judy. Look Don, I'm no expert. But I think you have to just do your best at loving, like practicing loving by making that the focus of every day. We need to practice with one another, being gentle, doing kind things, expressing gratitude. Stuff like that. I think it's about giving to one another rather than pushing for what we need to get from the other. I am not going to abort the baby because of your neediness. I mean, I do feel how fearful you are, but no! . . . I want to give myself, my whole body, to carrying this baby. And then to raising this baby with all my resources, physical, spiritual, intellectual. I don't know all the curveballs that life will throw our way, but no one does. And people do have children anyway and love them as best they can.

Don. Perhaps you are right. Perhaps all the excruciating self-doubt and fear amount to so many injuries and scars from my old man. And that was in the past. Now I am in the present with you—with pregnant you! Now I have an opportunity to make my own life an improvement on how my father did things. I suppose I am free to choose how I want to live and to love. I cannot do this alone, Judy. At a psychological level I am too damaged.

Judy. No one can do anything alone. We are creatures, damaged or broken in some way, and yet sustained by a kind of mercy, kindness, and generosity that is bigger than we are.

They join hands across the kitchen table, creating a circle of intimacy around the candle burning between them.

DISCUSSION OF DIFFERING METHODS OF CASE PRESENTATION

The first presentation and discussion of Judy's case is scholarly and is articulated in the voice of the third person observer, (despite the additional fact that the author was also Judy's friend). Although it is a narrative particular to Judy, it is presented in the language of an analytical pursuit of the universally true and righteous. The situation is described as though it were a (mathematical) problem: Don's history of having been victimized (variable x), and the pregnancy conflated with the victimizing power (variable y). The moral imperative is to solve the problem in terms of its variables. The problem articulated in terms of its variables leads to a solution or answer, metaphorically speaking, and that answer is abortion. In this approach, abortion remains an abstraction or an idea, the product of an equation, without any of the experiential dimension. Abortion becomes an even more attractive solution when the privileged cultural values of utility, practicality, and efficiency are added to the mix. The abortion is a kind of outcome that by means of syllogistic logic is readily

conflated with the true-in-general. I would also note the approach
to Don in terms of the science of psychology. "Can't Don get some
counselling?" says Laura. And Judy defends her position: "Let's face
it—given where he's at right now and how deep the roots of his problem lie, and the fact that he's never had counselling before, there's little chance that he could adjust to the idea of fatherhood by the time
a baby would arrive." A history of domestic violence is predicted to
beget more violence. Moreover, the presumption would appear to be
that Don must adjust to the idea of fatherhood. *The idea* or cognate,
fatherhood, is placed before *the experience* of having a baby. When
Judy speaks, she adopts the stance of one who is defending herself
in an argument of justification, as though she were the adjudicating
observer of herself. She does not expose her concealed interiority
with its own experiences of hurts and joys, fears and angers, etc. This
approach of the dispassionate analytical observer, who suppresses
the felt visceral interiority in favor of psychological norms, abstract
cognates, and problem-solving is the default position of those who
are trained in the medical sciences, indeed of many educated, reflective persons. The logic of cause-effect, i.e., the metanarrative of the
true-in-general, assumes that the suffering must be eradicated as a
pre-requisite for flourishing. Mystery has no place in this paradigm.
This familiar style of case presentation is summarized in table 1.

Table 1: Features of a Metanarrative of the True-in-General

- Scholarly format and language is used, showcasing ideas and prin-
  ciples that conflate the universally true and the morally right.
- Narration is by the third person observer.
- Experience is problematized: the facts at hand, e.g., pregnancy and
  domestic violence, become variables in an equation to be solved for
  moral righteousness.
- Intervention is essential, e.g., psychology with its abstract norms is a
  trusted mode of intervention.
- Abstract cognates are used, e.g., fatherhood, violence, pregnancy.
- There is a tone of defensiveness, justification, conflict, and argument.
- Joys, fears, angers, etc. remain concealed. Visceral resonance is
  suppressed.

In the second presentation, the format of the text is more like a dramatic dialogue (which I imagined and wrote) than like an abstract equation. The situation is set on a stage and the plot moves from suffering towards flourishing through the dialogue of the players. This is accomplished by means of the grammatical voice of the first person (plural), the sufferers, in this case Judy and Don. They expose to one another their deepest hurts and desires, i.e., the imprints of their lived experiences that give meaning to the circumstances at hand. The longing for a child and the fear of the responsibility that this involves come together without the intention of a solution or a fix. The tension is hard and uncomfortable. This is acknowledged and held gently between them. The tone is one of intimacy and embrace, not argument and defensiveness. In this presentation, the pregnancy is an experience, and fatherhood is a related experience, to be lived out and grown into with all the difficulties and the joys. In this alternative style of discourse, pregnancy and parenthood as lived personal experiences need not be submitted to scrutiny and authentication by universal psychological norms. Don and Judy are seen as capable agents of their own flourishing. They need not be victims of an (ill-founded) imperative to eradicate suffering. The embrace of new life and the daunting enormity of the commitment does not eradicate one's past lived experience of annihilating violence. In contrast to the prevailing secular paradigm depicted in the first case presentation, the pre-requisite for new-found vitality and flourishing is not the eradication of evil by the autonomous self and its colleagues.

The pre-requisite for flourishing is to turn away from a pre-occupation with the hurts of evil and to attend instead to one's participation in that ineffable mystery of largesse, generosity, kindness, and compassion. In other words, one elects to participate in newness of life and renewed vitality, turning away from the futile project of eradicating experiences of annihilation. This participation engages the realm of mystery. The meaning-making symbols that convey such mystery are words, objects, and relationships. The dialogue between Judy and Don could also be understood as a dialogue between two parts of the self, the competent executive self and the vulnerable inner self. Meaning-making, not problem-solving, becomes the issue at hand: harm and flourishing, annihilation and animation. The candle might symbolize vitality in the context of the empirical facts that seem to point towards ruin. The relationship of intimate, kind embrace between the dialogue partners may symbolize the closeness of that life-giving sacred Presence. It is through symbol and metaphor that the human being gropes towards meaning, in contrast to the language of de-mystification, which aims at causal analyses, solutions, and classifications.

The role of the clinician in the second presentation does not involve the formulation of moral imperatives and principles. When (and if) the deeply transformative dialogue is shared with the clinician, the professional role might be that of a facilitator, who formulates carefully phrased questions when the dialogue stalls or seems to get side-tracked into analyses, moral oughts/shoulds, and problem-solving. The work of the facilitator is to coax the narrative along, inviting the voice of the first person to speak and to continue speaking. The facilitator also learns to identify movements that hinder or support healing shifts in identity. Note that in the example provided, I condensed the circumstances into a short dialogue to illustrate the features of this alternative style of discourse. But in real life the dialogue around mystery will unfold gradually over time—weeks, months, even all the years of a life-time. There will be forays into what the clinical observer might identify as moral wrongs or as psychological and somatic illness: marital breakdown, an abortion, depression, recurrent respiratory infections, abdominal pains without diagnostic markers, fibromyalgia, etc. The somatic illnesses require intervention, as much as is medically possible; the psycho-somatic dysfunctionalities call for the respect that one accords mystery. That ineffable part is the locus of the suffering. On this view, the facilitator's role is to listen for the overall direction of movement from suffering to flourishing, companioning the shifts in identity from victim of violence, hurt, and annihilation to agent of flourishing, wellbeing, and newness of life.

The second method of case presentation illustrates the proposed metanarrative of becoming well, involving the healing transformation of advance from suffering victim towards empowered agent. This style of discourse features the voice of the first person, a

non-conflictual tone of relational intimacy, sensed visceral respons-
es, imaginative metaphors, and the very experience of a renewed
vitality. A metanarrative of becoming well has the potential for a
more nuanced relationship between patient and healthcare professional. It does not displace a metanarrative of the true-in-general,
which undergirds the process of competent diagnostics. The proposed metanarrative of becoming well supports the mystery of ontological becoming (rather than critical, analytic de-mystification)
in both teller and listener.

Table 2: Features of a Metanarrative of Becoming Well-in-Particular

- Voice of the "I"—the sufferer—speaks.
- Experience is conveyed as a narrative of suffering, e.g., pregnancy, fatherhood, domestic violence.
- Tone is intimate, gentle, and relational.
- Subjective visceral feelings are exposed, e.g., anger, fear, doubt, aversion, longing, etc.
- Uncertainty and mystery are acceptable.
- Symbols and metaphors are used to suggest meaning.
- The emphasis is upon movement, transformation, and identity shifts.
- Problem-solving and interventions (e.g., psychological or medical) are de-emphasized.

CONCLUSIONS AND CLINICAL APPLICATION

In this chapter I have integrated themes from the medical humanities and from the theological literature. When narrative is regarded
as a medium of becoming free in response to suffering, then the
potential for healing transformation may unfold. But such movement is not amenable to empirical observation; it is a dynamic of
the concealed human interiority. To speak of transformative movement, i.e., to narrate one's experience of movement, away from the
victim identity towards a free agent of flourishing, is to engage the
realm of mystery. To communicate around mystery requires symbol and metaphor, a linguistic style with which professionals in the
sciences and, more generally, persons in a secular society are usually neither familiar nor skillful. I have illustrated this approach,

with its embrace of mystery and meaning-making, for the clinical setting by making use of the dramatic dialogue form of discourse. I have summarized and specified the details of such a narrative and propose to call it a metanarrative of becoming well.

I have contrasted this metanarrative of the ineffable human process of becoming with an approach that we are more familiar with, namely, that of the problem-solving, analytic rationality. This analytic approach also tells a story, but it is a story of scientific de-mystification that aims for the return to or the recovery of an externally determined static norm or benchmark. The agent is the observer/clinician, and the patient is the object under observation. The patient remains passive vis à vis the interiority; transformation is not the goal. Agency is limited to choosing between institutions, care-givers, and interventions, with the expectation that well-being will follow after a restored alignment with universal norms. The patient's experience of a personal human interiority has no place in this paradigm. The professionals who provide this approach and the patients who expect it generally have a world view in which the body is regarded as a mechanism that requires fixing when broken. If there is any meaning-making at all around good and evil, it re-volves around external universal norms, with no appreciation that there might be a need for more nuance. Flourishing/suffering, free moral agency in the face of suffering, and healing transformation towards flourishing are aspects of being human that are inadmis-sible in this (prevailing) paradigm. This secular, science-based ap-proach, characterized by de-mystification and problematization, I refer to as a metanarrative of the true-in-general.

SUMMARY

I have argued that there is a need for two kinds of metanarratives in healthcare, one which has a repertoire of interventions with proven success in restoring the normal (the Metanarrative of True-in-Gen-eral), and one which follows a narrative tradition with powerful symbols that express the ineffable process of felt sensory movement from suffering to wellbeing (the Metanarrative of Becoming Well).

While narrative is increasingly highlighted in medical practice, the characteristics of that narrative have not yet been specified. In chapter 3, I have begun this process of specification of a narrative with the potential for healing transformation. While this kind of metanarrative is perhaps less essential to the theoretician, both scientific and moral, it is the professional who is attending the sufferer that will appreciate its significance. The Metanarrative of Becoming Well provides a unique linguistic vehicle for the expression of experiences of the ineffable, which are, in fact, experiences of suffering and flourishing and the movements between them.

In chapter 4, I will bring the reader's focus away from narratives of suffering and into a narrative of flourishing. While the Christian doctrinal tradition uses the term, Resurrection, for the notion of an after-life of beatific flourishing, my intention will be to sketch out at an experiential level the intensification of vitality so powerful that it takes one beyond the state of suffering into a state of flourishing where ultimately there is eternally no more hurt.

4

Beyond Suffering and the Endless
Cycles of Destruction

In chapter 1, I outlined the pre-modern understanding of human
nature as a potential alternate to the scientific understanding of
human physiology, psychology, and sociology. I developed a descriptive definition of suffering in terms of suppressed movement
towards the good, i.e., immobilization—"stuckness"—in the not-
so-good. In chapter 2, I further elaborated this paradigm of movement. In terms of movement, the goal is to come "unstuck" and to
experience a freedom of movement towards the good. In chapter 3,
I showed how narrative can be the linguistic tool to describe and
indeed to enable a mysterious movement of transformation so profound that it is essentially an ontological re-creating; the mute, paralyzed victim of oppression becomes a free agent with the unlikely
yet real capacity to participate divine movement. The imprinted
hurt is not adjudicated as culpability but is instead subverted by
ordering the passions towards a deeply held hope for wellbeing. My
intention has been to distinguish between the well-studied intellectual nature and the less studied sensory nature, with emphasis

upon the latter as being not only the locus of hurt, suffering, and death, but also the locus of the concupiscible and irascible passions that have the potential to compel us beyond the afflictions.

In this chapter, our exploration of the sensory nature will continue; the focus will be the movement of resting in the good attained, i.e., the capacity in the sensory nature for contemplation. The contemplative stance of resting or abiding with the felt sensibilities is essential when reality is experienced as a dynamic gradient from suffering towards flourishing. On this view, the contemplative attitude of one's physicality enables a receptive cooperation with the penetration of healing grace into those deep interior recesses of sensory nature that are imprinted with hurt.

The question to be addressed is this: How does a sufferer, who is, by my definition, shut down in terms of the movements of the passions, experience a desire or passion for flourishing? And how can this desire come about in a world that predicts with persuasive logic the futility of ultimate wellbeing, proving again and again, with empirical certainty, nothing but endless cycles of violence, disintegration, and death? Those formed in the Christian tradition might respond that it is the will that must be configured to the eternal good through faith and scholarship in order to overcome the evidence-based claims of modernity.

While this approach is indeed a proven and authentic experience of the tradition, I will argue that to configure the will exclusively through the imperatives of faith and the critiques of an analytical mind is insufficient and indeed potentially even a hindrance to the attainment of the good—when the context is an *experience at the sensory level* of the not-so-good. I will develop the position that in the context of suffering, referred to as dysphoria in certain contexts, contemplation is a process that necessarily involves one's physicality, with its sensibilities and its longings around pleasure and hurt. Healing from the bondage of recurrent experiences of hurt is an experience accessible via the habit of resting in a felt sense of pleasure, safety, happiness, and contentment, in other words, sensory experiences of the good. Furthermore, healing is the experience of undergoing an ineffable transformation whereby there is the progressive subversion of those specific hurtful realities that stifle a felt sense of the good. This healing transformation of the sensory physicality confers upon the sufferer the freedom for a felt sense of all things good, pleasant, delightful, and joyful. Thus, in the context of the struggle to advance from suffering towards flourishing, the habit of contemplation is not only a habit of the intellect and will but also a habit of the sensibilities and longings within the sufferer's human corporeality.

SUFFERING: PROFESSIONALLY OBSERVED OR VICARIOUSLY EXPERIENCED?

One approach to suffering is to observe the sufferer; such observations are often collected under the cognate term, suffering. Eric Cassell wrote on suffering from the perspective of the professional, medical observer, noting that personhood became ruptured by the losses that came with the loss of health. When such things as job, spousal relationship, friends, prestige, or societal role were lost, one's personhood appeared to be ruptured. His description was that of a highly sensitive doctor, who articulated his observations, as most doctors do, in the language of science, according to what was generally found to be true.[1] In other words, his approach was from above. Although he may have felt some resonance with the sufferer's situation, experiencing perhaps his own subjective response to the sufferer, this aspect was not articulated. It is not customary to assign importance to a subjectivity that participates vicariously in the patient's suffering; science admits as valid only that which is objective and empirical. The part that is not science—the art of care-giving—has its own specifications, which require our attention.

Thomas Aquinas noted that the threat to wellbeing posed by the proximity of evil called forth a response in the physicality of the person apprehending the threat. He called these sensed "corporeal transmutations" the deep passions: love, hate, sorrow, anger, fear, courage, despair, and hope.[2] What the ancient mind introduced (and what the post-modern mind is perhaps re-discovering) is

1. Cassell, *Nature of Suffering.*
2. ST I-II.25.

that these passions are bodily transformations or movements in response to an experience of suffering, whereby the human being is moved to pursue wellness. In other words, the passions are a response of the sensory nature to some alluring good thing (wellness /flourishing), which can only be attained by a difficult struggle with obstacles or threats to wellbeing (imprinted experiences of hurt and suffering). When the evil, i.e., experiences of suffering, harm, or hurt, threatens to the point of overwhelming the passions, the movements of response are immobilized, and even the vocal apparatus becomes paralyzed and mute. Thomas observed that this state of *torpor* hindered creaturely movement towards its destiny of beatific flourishing.[3] Similar to Thomas's torpor is Dorothee Soelle's description of a mute, numb state—the deepest degree of suffering—in which one moves only by rote at the command of the oppressor, incapable of excitement, lament, fear, or hope, let alone creativity.[4] She was describing the apathy that afflicts the citizen of political modernity. Informed by these sources, I will use the term suffering to signify the experience of muteness and paralysis in the wake of overwhelming harm.

Cassell, Soelle, and Aquinas were *observers* of suffering. My goal is to take our understanding of suffering beyond the perspective of the observer. I seek to understand suffering through the lens of the sufferer. This demands that I be prepared *to experience* what the sufferer is going through; my project thus becomes an exercise in vicarious suffering. Vicarious suffering is what turns the approach upside down and from below.

In desiring to experience vicarious suffering, I first desire *to feel* my own suffering, to re-collect hurtful experiences at the level of my own physical sensibilities. This is not to be conflated with a sado-masochistic desire to inflict suffering upon myself. It is to intentionally pursue an awareness of the aggregated, experiential knowing of the sensory interiority, which Thomas has described in terms of the interior senses. The memory of the interior senses retains imprints of pleasure and wellbeing as well as of harm and

3. ST I-II.35.8.
4. Soelle, *Suffering*.

hurt. The body remembers and responds so as to avoid destruction, to survive, to reproduce, and indeed to thrive. In animals
this intelligence is the instinct: "This is a predator, not a mate!
This is poisonous and not good to eat!" The animal using its instinct does not think or weigh the odds; its movement arises from
a physically sensed knowing of the external milieu as harmful or
helpful to its wellbeing. The human animal has a parallel physical
process of knowing, which Thomas has called the cogitative sense/
particular reason, an interior sense of the sensory/bodily nature. In
other words, the body has its own "smarts," quite distinct from the
syllogistic thinking of the intellectual nature. Of course, the unity
of the sensory and intellectual natures means that the intellectual
nature is continually informed by the meanings of potential harm
or wellness apprehended by the sensory nature; the intellectual capacities of judging, choosing, deciding, etc. arise from and operate
"in synch with" the configuration of the interior senses of sensory
nature. It is therefore essential to the project of vicarious suffering
that the intellect become conscious of the primal rationality of sensory nature from whence all the vital movements, as well as the
hindrances to vitality, have their beginnings.

In a tradition that understands the world to be hierarchical
and sees things "from above," i.e., through the intellect's capacity
of cognition, the passions have been understood in terms of the
cognates, evil and good. But as *cognates*, evil and good have become
conflated with right and wrong, severed off from the *experiences* of
suffering and wellbeing. To experience my own suffering—the imprints of particular evils upon me—requires that I suspend the use
of evil and good as terms of abstract universals and work with my
own particular experiences of hurt and delight. In the view from
above, universal principles or ideas of right and wrong provide the
lens for interpreting particular experiences of hurt and of wellbeing. By contrast, the view from below affords us the understanding
of lived experience as a narrative; there is a story of suffering and
death that can open up to resurrected eternal life. On this view, some
experiences are life-depleting, paralyzing, and silencing, i.e., bad/
evil, while others are life-giving, inspire one's creativity, and inten-
sify one's felt sense of wellbeing, i.e., good. Experience can become

life-giving even in the context of the difficult process of dying. This experiential felt sense of animation or of annihilation—the good and the bad—introduces a possible critique of the intellectual habit of classifying experiences as right and wrong.

In the Christian faith tradition, one speaks about life—its intensification and its attenuation—in narratives with symbolic meaning rather than in terms of science (as in physiology and psychology). This approach allows one to speak about those ineffable aspects of lived experience that escape the rationality of science. The incarnation, life, passion, death, and resurrection of Christ appeal not to the analytic, scientific capacities of our minds, but to the gut feelings of our sensory nature. To appeal to the sensory nature is to engage that part of a human being that cries and laughs, loves and hates, fears and hopes, feels hurt and feels good, etc. In other words, the passions of a human being are ordered towards the ever-intensifying vitality of participating the divine, but they are at the same time susceptible to an external milieu that may obstruct and not support this advance towards ultimate wellbeing. The resurrection narratives become the storied symbolic rationality that confers upon our experiences of suffering a horizon of ultimate wellbeing with no more suffering. The resurrection narratives express an experience of overwhelming vitality in the context of death's empirical certainty. According to Brian Robinette, the resurrection narratives were and still are stories that overwhelm the sensibilities of one's human corporeality. Whereas previously evil/suffering were *the* overwhelming experiences, the resurrection introjects an experience of feeling overwhelmed by good/wellbeing.[5] In the context of lived experiences of suffering and annihilation, the resurrection-experience signifies overwhelming, ineffable animation. The emphasis here is upon the resurrection as sensory experience and not as intellectual cognate. While the latter is communicated in the analytic discourses of science, the former calls forth the narrative language of metaphor and symbol.

When analytic discourse eclipses narrative symbolism there is potential for amplifying the hurt by obscuring the horizon of

---

5. Robinette, *Grammars of Resurrection.*

wellbeing. When the analytic intellectual nature becomes disconnected from sensory nature's felt pleasures and visceral aversions, then it takes upon itself a peculiar (wrongheaded) "freedom," i.e., a power, to judge and to inflict penalty, justifying such process as valuable learning for an erring corporeality. However, true learning comes not from externally imposed punishments, but rather from one's inner sensibilities applied *by the self* to the consequences of one's comportment. The interior senses of sensory nature *feel* hurt / delight and this knowing compels comportment accordingly. However, when the inescapable externally imposed punishments amount to immobilization and silencing, then the experience of suffering is amplified and perpetuated. The felt sense—allure or aversion—becomes disabled and muted by the overwhelming power in the penalties. A colloquial speaker might use such expressions as "numbed out" or "petrified." With the silencing of one's interior sensibilities (the apprehensions), the desires or passions (the appetitions) are also disabled. Soelle calls this state, apathy. Felt possibilities around agency for creative change are shut down by the rote habits of a victim identity.[6] The intellect of critical analyses and adjudications continues to function, but the nuanced *sensibilities* that flesh out the thinking mind into a robust human intelligence are missing.

The professional (healthcare, education, law, etc.) falls into this predicament when the analytic habits of the mind crowd out and silence the narrative symbolism of one's own laments and longings. This silencing deep within is what may call forth a contemplative, groping towards healing and ultimate wellbeing. As one's personal, sensory interiority awakens from habits of silencing and immobilization, the cries, the angers, the hopes, the fears, the loves, and the hates begin to assert themselves. This is the nature of the contemplative process that matures the consciousness for the visceral resonance of vicarious suffering.

6. Soelle, *Suffering*, 75.

CONTEMPLATION: AN ARDUOUS
ATTENTIVENESS

The awakening of the sensory interiority, with its laments and its longings, is the stuff of vicarious suffering unfolding into mutual wellbeing, a kind of shared state of flourishing in which suffering is subverted. The attitude or disposition that is coherent with or suited to this ultimate state of wellbeing is contemplation. In the context of suffering, contemplation may be regarded as a refining of the disposition of sensory nature, which at a primal level seeks pleasure and avoids harm. Thomas (relying upon Aristotle) describes "a special natural habit" which provides the human being with "first practical principles" (as opposed to the speculative principles, which are also a habitual way of understanding). To attend to the sensed first principles around what affirms and what harms one's being is called synderesis. Synderesis "is said to incite to the good and murmur at evil." Around this specification of synderesis, the second objection posed by Thomas suggests that sensuality, i.e., the sensory nature, and synderesis are opposed. But Thomas replies that although individual acts may indeed be opposed, it nevertheless remains true that to distinguish what is good and what is evil represents a broader capacity of the *integrated* sensory and intellectual aspects of human nature.[7] In the context of suffering, which has its locus in the sensory nature, the role of the sensual sensory nature in synderesis becomes relevant. Even in the silences and paralyses of suffering, the sensory nature retains its experiential awareness of what hurts and what pleases—the meaning of synderesis.

Sensory experiences of what hurts and what pleases fall outside the realm of logical justification and empirical proof. A body knows without proof when it feels bad and when things feel good. This awareness—this experiential certainty—that something is good or bad for the self is cultivated and further nuanced by means of a contemplative immersion in the supreme good/God. Participating the ineffable with a contemplative disposition of the sensual sensory body engages the feelings of wellness and of harm, and those feelings come to the surface in stories. Arising from a contemplative

7. ST I.79.12.2.

disposition, the work of the stories is to grope beyond the empirical reality towards more nuanced layers of possible meaning.[8] These narratives and their metaphors also find expression in a choreography of rational and particular movements, which cohere with the interior senses—memory, imagination, and meaning (*intentiones*)—in distinguishing harm from good *in the body*. This choreography of movements, in its particularity, does not necessarily cohere with every moral principle of the true in general.[9] Synderesis viewed from below is more a linguistic groping into contingency than a deductive process of analytic, intellectual ordering. In the context of companioning a sufferer, the attending observer engages the view from below, allowing the sophisticated interior senses of his own corporeal interiority to resonate. Through this "faculty" of visceral resonance one participates in the moral groping towards new choreographies of action. This visceral resonance, expressed as a contemplative storied groping for wellness is also the dynamic of synderesis. Synderesis, thus understood, becomes the basis of an approach to the art of facilitating a sufferer's advance towards flourishing. Visceral resonance in the observer, whether the clinician or the moralist, is sensory subjectivity ordered to the synderesis of distinguishing harm from good. On this view, subjectivity can no longer be understood as that which must be suppressed in the interest of truth-telling objectivity. To dwell subjectively in that deeply felt sense of anther's distress is the difficult work of moral discernment. What move is to be made that will afford the sufferer freedom for the advance towards wellbeing and the emergence from the bondage of suffering?

In the next few paragraphs I will use a published article to illustrate differences in methodology—from above vs from below—in approaching a moral dilemma. I will refer to an article on gender dysphoria, but *not* to engage in problem-solving issues around gender but rather to highlight two possible methods of approaching

8. Botha, *Metaphor and Its Moorings*.

9. "The more we descend to matters of detail, the more frequently we encounter defects. . . . In matters of action, truth or practical rectitude are not the same for all. . . . And where there is the same rectitude in matters of detail, it is not equally known to all" (ST I-II. 94.4).

the suffering/dysphoria. I wish to show the various ways that these two approaches may co-exist: conflate, complement, confound, compete, etc. I wish to show that it becomes important to a fulsome ethics discourse to identify the approach from above and the approach from below as it is at work in any given moment of deliberation.

In a recent article that explores the way forward for those suffering from gender dysphoria, Scott Bader-Saye contrasts the method from above and the approach from below.[10] He is not intentional about this process of contrast, but I believe that it is methodologically important. In the following paragraphs, using his essay, I will highlight the contrast between a *moral observer*, who logically justifies principles that are true-in-general, and the *sufferer* (in this case of gender dysphoria), who gropes through narrative for a way to feel better. The article illustrates that the moral dilemma around gender dysphoria may be considered in terms of cognates (from above) and/or in terms of the sufferer's experience (from below). Both are important and both are valid. Both of these two approaches merit consideration as distinct and complementary approaches that need not exert a kind of moral supremacy of one over the other.

Bader-Saye sets up his discussion of the moral tension by describing first the principles-in-question (an approach possibly modelled on the Objections with which Thomas Aquinas introduces each of his questions.) I will summarize these Objections:

1. "Transgender identity presupposes a Gnostic retreat from the unity of the body and soul and the goodness of materiality."[11] In response to the trans person who feels "like a man trapped in a woman's body," John Milbank, a proponent of non-Gnostic dualism, states, "Bodily appearances of engenderment are no longer seen as manifestations of a psychic-bodily unity, but as meaningless physical circumstances."[12]

2. "Gender transitioning is a denial of and a threat to the fixed ontological male/female binary built into creation and affirmed

10. Bader-Saye, "Transgender Body's Grace," 75–92.

11. Bader-Saye, "Transgender Body's Grace," 80.

12. Milbank quoted in Bader-Saye, "Transgender Body's Grace," 81.

in Genesis 1:27."[13] Oliver O'Donovan views this binary of gender as a divine gift, which the transgender person rejects.[14] In fact, Milbank observes that the transgender person is part of an illegitimate initiative "to abolish gender altogether."[15]

3. "Gender fluidity involves a capitulation to the idol of modern voluntarism and self-creation at the expense of embracing natural limits and human ecology."[16] O'Donovan affirms this perspective, recognizing that the body is "not only a vehicle for the free expression of our spirits, but also a given structure and meaning which limits freedom."[17] Milbank views the cult of transgenderism as "a manifestation of rejected liberalism."[18]

The common feature of these three "Objections" to the cognate, transgender, is that they are deduced by an approach "from above." All of these statements can be justified and defended as universally true abstract ideas. Such abstract statements about the true-in-general characterize a discourse from above in which the statements become external norms of righteousness. If we use transgender as an example, transgender becomes an abstract cognate and an objectified state of transgression against three logically defensible moral norms. Although the Objections allow for rare exceptions to the rules, the moral discourse used in stating the Objections does not give voice to visceral resonance in the observer, let alone to the voice of the sufferer. A discourse of cognates in pursuit of truth and righteousness proceeds from above; the approach from below involves the voicing of dysphoria as a felt experience. A fulsome ethics discourse requires both perspectives, but in the tradition of moral philosophy/theology it is not clear what the narrative "from below" ought to look like in order to be found morally relevant.

After the above statements of the universally true, Bader-Saye sets out the narratives of dysphoria (suffering) in the voices of those

13. Bader-Saye, "Transgender Body's Grace," 81.

14. O'Donovan, "Transexualism," 143.

15. Milbank quoted in Bader-Saye, "Transgender Body's Grace," 81.

16. Bader-Saye, "Transgender Body's Grace," 81.

17. O'Donovan quoted in Bader-Saye, "Transgender Body's Grace," 82.

18. Milbank quoted in Bader-Saye, "Transgender Body's Grace," 82.

who tell the story of a hurt-filled experience of eros, or what we refer to culturally as gender dysphoria. The voice of the sufferer who experiences the gender dysphoria becomes an audible counterpoint to the voice of the observer who articulates the universal principles; here I am contrasting the first person and the third person grammatical voicing. The suffering of feeling invisible is a common trope among self-descriptions of transgendered persons. "Manning spoke regularly, and with despair, of feeling 'poisoned' by the testosterone in her body and of a ghostlike invisibility: . . . what use was living?"[19] Arin Andrews, a transgender teenager, describes his inability to communicate his real self. "They all think I am someone I'm not. . . . Stuck inside this . . . thing. . . . I hate it. . . . Being alive isn't worth this."[20] To help interpret the narratives, Bader-Saye cites Rowan Williams, who notes that such invisibility thwarts reciprocity, which in turn obstructs grace. Drawing upon the novel, *Raj Quartet* by Paul Scott, Williams writes, "In a particularly unpromising sexual encounter, [the heroine] is described as having 'entered her body's grace.'" Williams puts a positive emphasis upon the body and its desiring. "There may have been little love, even little generosity, in Sarah's lovemaking, but she has discovered that her body can be the cause of happiness to her and to another."[21] The story of the desires and longings is about her sensory nature re-awakening from its previously stifled and immobilized state. For Williams, desire is key; "God desires us, *as if we were God*, as if we were that unconditional response of God's giving that God's self makes up in the life of the Trinity. We are created so that we may be caught up in this."[22] These chaotic movements of sensory nature and its difficult longings for wellbeing are rendered invisible when the approach to morality is exclusively from above. When we listen to the voice of the sufferer, we come to understand that to be hurting and to be wrong are not synonymous; on the other hand, to be hurt and to be wronged *are* more closely related. The view from above works with

---

19. Shaer quoted in Bader-Saye, "Transgender Body's Grace," 85.

20. Andrews quoted in Bader-Saye, "Transgender Body's Grace," 85.

21. Williams quoted in Bader-Saye, "Transgender Body's Grace," 84.

22. Williams quoted in Bader-Saye, "Transgender Body's Grace," 84.

the cognate, transgender, while the view from below works with the experience of dysphoria/suffering.

Bader-Saye cites Thomas Nagel to further elaborate the two contrasting ways of approaching moral tension: the morality of erotic desire may be more along the lines of subjectivity and particularity (from below), and not well-suited to a paradigm (from above) of objective observations and universal truths. "There is no clear, distinct, internal *subject* who comes to know the inert, external *object* of the body as one's own; rather, we come to know ourselves *in toto* as embodied creatures in the many small and mundane interactions of daily life by which we encounter the gaze, the touch, the words, the gestures of others as they engage us."[23] To recognize the importance of perceiving such encounters is to acknowledge that the sensory nature cannot be conflated with intellection around principles. A love story, when analyzed in terms of moral principles, loses its erotic sensory quality. This capacity of the sensory nature fully alive is what ultimately knows the felt sense of good and of evil—of wellness and of harm. This is what moral awareness looks like from below.

Bader-Saye also cites Sarah Coakley's work on religious symbolism and erotic desiring. I interpret Coakley's work as a further example of potential linguistic methodology available to the sufferer, as he/she voices a narrative of experience (i.e., the perspective from below). She gropes for understanding of erotic desiring through religious symbolism and not through static universal principles that would impose upon the sexes a kind of classic ordering. Her approach is to situate these questions into the context of a developing capacity to participate in the triune God. In other words, she avoids a paradigm in which transgender is the object under critical analytic observation. Instead, her focus is upon the protagonist or sufferer, who, in her view, may inscribe his desiring into a symbolic (religious) metanarrative. Such narrative process re-orders and indeed restores the dysphoric protagonist's desiring towards a "journey[ing] with the Holy Spirit of unpredictable

---

23. Bader-Saye, "Transgender Body's Grace," 84.

transformation."[24] Coakley's method retains erotic desiring as *an experience* of one's human longing for God. It is thus a suitable approach for the narrative voicing of the sufferer's dysphoria. By staying with the experience, she avoids getting caught up in the cognate, transgender, from a world of classic binary understanding and is able to offer a re-description of desire and of gender that introduces the notion of "labile."

> We come to know how to handle sex and gender rightly not by reading a natural order directly off our bodies, but by subjecting our bodies to the discipline necessary to enact our movement into divine love and to share that love with the world. In other words, bodies, sex, and gender are not ends in themselves, nor are they static realities with predetermined meanings; rather, they are relativized by divine desire and so attain a malleability by which they can be reformed, transformed, and ordered to their higher end.[25]

Building upon symbols from the Christian faith tradition (informed by her scholarship in Gregory of Nyssa), she offers the image of gender trickling or flowing into an eschaton in which only our "ontological humanness will remain" and gender will be transformed into "differentiated relational being." The new gendering will be "labile to the logic and flow of trinitarian, divine desire"; it will become "mysterious . . . [with a] plastic openness to divine transformation."[26] When gender dysphoria is thus inscribed into the language of our religious symbolism (God as Trinity), desire, including erotic desiring, remains personal, subjective, mysterious, and legitimate. When the voice from below is enabled, the gender dysphoric sufferer is released from the hurtful, judgemental statements generated when universals are intellectually positioned as the norms and benchmarks of goodness.[27] Such release into *freedom*

24. Coakley quoted in Bader-Saye, "Transgender Body's Grace," 87.

25. Coakley quoted in Bader-Saye, "Transgender Body's Grace," 87.

26. Coakley quoted in Bader-Saye, "Transgender Body's Grace," 88.

27. Having established that the physical, human body, with its longings and erotic desiring as well as its dysphoria from both invisibility and adjudication, is potentially the locus of graced transformation, Bader-Saye makes an

from hurt calls forth a *freedom for* participating in the desire of God. When the view from below reveals an advancing into freedom, then the movements of human desiring—erotic or otherwise—acquire delicacy and moral nuance.

A practical example of this contemplative focusing of the desiring sensory body is to be found in the Ignatian tradition of spirituality. The spiritual exercises offer a contemplative immersion of the whole sensory nature, both the apprehensive interior senses and the appetitive passions, into the life, suffering, death, and res- urrection of Christ, i.e., into the incarnate presence of God.[28] A contemporary articulation of this Ignatian tradition has coined the term Bio-Spirituality, referring to the practice of awareness of the "felt-sense" that can be perceived "underneath" the cognitions and emotions; I interpret this perception of the felt sense as a referenc- ing of the sensory nature.[29] Referring to 1 Cor 12:27 (about the body of Christ), we read that it is important

---

unexpected move: "Those who transform the body through hormones and surgery do so in order to present the self in a unified manner, and in so doing they make a partner of the body for the sake of grace—that is for seeing and being seen 'as significant, as wanted,' and 'as the occasion of joy'" (Bader-Saye, "Transgender Body's Grace," 89). Having practiced endocrinology for forty years, I wish to point out that at the level of strict evidence-based medicine, surgical and hormonal interventions in gender dysphoria have not been found to alter the rates of suicide in the affected population and are regarded as a sci- entifically unfounded mutilation (see Laidlaw et al., "Endocrine Treatment"). Profound transformation is the work of graced desiring, not medicine. In medicine, the goal is to restore a body to universal physiologic and anatomic norms. And norms, be they physiologic, anatomic, or moral, indicate the view from above. Gender dysphoria, like many other kinds of suffering, is not re- lieved by the view from above with its skilled medical interventions and moral principles. Gender dysphoria challenges us to tread gently, with a distinctly different approach, which I have called attending the sufferer. By recognizing that the view from above is merely complementary to the dysphoric experi- ence from below, the imperative to intervene in the dysphoria and/or to restore moral norms is softened. Softening means that both the sufferer and the at- tending companion become free for the narrative and the symbols that grope for the mysterious flourishing and wellbeing of resurrection.

28. Puhl, *Spiritual Exercises of St Ignatius.*

29. Campbell and McMahon, *Bio-Spirituality.*

to explore your own inner feelings, to *touch and feel* your way through your own body rather than always trying to think or figure everything out in your head. You balance your thinking by turning to *a different kind of habit* for guidance, a habit which involves putting your analyzing problem-solving mind on the shelf periodically in order more attentively to notice, nurture, and hold in a caring way the felt-senses within your body. You make space each day for regular check in time, discovering what stories might lie in waiting in your feelings and felt-senses. This more physical task also includes noticing *where* you carry a problem or issue in your body and how this actually feels.[30]

Contemplation is thus described as a habit of attending the bodily sensations, an attention that immerses the praying sufferer into that sacred dynamic of incarnate longing and loving. To see the self as the self is seen by God, a self that is real, is good, and is beautiful, is the arduous experience at the core of a contemplative stance. It is this contemplative habit of the sensory nature that enables the sufferer, be it gender dysphoria or any other type of dysphoria, to advance towards a felt sense of legitimacy and wellbeing, free from the distractions and pain of medicine's pharmacologic and surgical manipulations and free also from the classifications and adjudications according to moral norms. The advance from dysphoria towards wellbeing leads in due time to the *telos* of beatitude, an advance that is graced with a freedom for flourishing while at the same time an arduous process of coming free from the bondage of suffering.

FLOURISHING

In this section I will characterize flourishing as a resurrection dynamic that subverts suffering. Like suffering, flourishing will be understood as an experience, not an abstraction from experience. The experience is one of release from the bondage or immobilization brought about by overwhelming evil. It is an experience of union, or at least intimacy, with the desired good, free from the threat of

30. Campbell and McMahon, *Bio-Spirituality,* 123.

being sabotaged, hurt, or harmed by evil. Flourishing thus depends upon a certain configuration of the imagination. It depends also upon a particular kind of freedom. When understood as a resurrection dynamic, flourishing requires a particular kind of discourse, namely, symbolic narrative and metaphor. This kind of discourse is distinguished from the analytic logic of philosophic argument and scientific problem-solving.

The Pauline metaphor of the seed undergoing transformation into a fruit is used to imaginatively probe (rather than to critically analyze) the transformative dynamic of resurrection. For Brian Robinette, this metaphor means that "the spiritual body is at once continuous and discontinuous with our present state of existence."[31] He suggests that sin is what prevents the corruptible Pauline "flesh and blood" from entering the eschaton. This "flesh and blood" state of our physicality is the bondage and immobilization that I have called suffering. The somatic reality of resurrection is not an anthropological phenomenon but rather something not yet experienced. Whereas at first the body lives "under its own power," as it comes increasingly "under the influence of God's Spirit [it becomes] a new somatic reality."[32] The resurrection of the body is a dynamic process whereby Holy Spirit infuses increasing vitality of being—wellbeing—into the body; Spirit does not work to disappear the bodily materiality. Indeed, as in Bader-Saye's fine discussion, the soul's longing to be loved into wellbeing is a dynamic with the potential to subvert the human pain of being invisible, illegitimate, and adjudicated. The experience of invisibility or illegitimacy is not unique to issues around gender. A human being who experiences a condemnation to invisibility and illegitimacy is experiencing overwhelming, terminal evil, in which the physicality of the passions becomes immobilized (literally petrified) by the fear. The converse is the resurrection dynamic of longing to be well, to love, and to flourish. The condemnation to invisibility is annihilating; the longing to be loved is a potentially transformative dynamic of resurrection.

31. Robinette, *Grammars of Resurrection*, 153.
32. Robinette, *Grammars of Resurrection*, 157.

The flourishing, soul-filled body of the resurrection comes of the subversion of evil rather than of conquest. To flourish is to arrive at that place of primal peace, which does *not* mean a state of suppressed chaos. Resurrection experiences of flourishing in this life do not come of a violent power-over or conquering of another. Flourishing comes of participating God's merciful, life-giving justice in response to the harm or evil that has enveloped, imprinted, and configured the sufferer. In contradistinction to a belief system shaped by the logic of a "fight against evil," the God of Judeo-Christian Scripture creates and inspires a radically new vitality in the context of personal suffering. "God's response is non-reciprocal to what precipitates it. God does not apply violence to violence, force to force, tit for tat, but rather overcomes sin through eschatological pardon, violence through agapic hospitality, and death through the renewal of life."[33] On this view, a sacred vindication of the sufferer engages in the struggle to recognize and to name the perpetrator of hurt. But, rather than wreaking a justice of vengeance, the justice of the resurrection "reaches out with loving vulnerability to the persecutor in a profound gesture of embrace, with the aim that the persecutor be converted and reconciled to [the] victim as the concrete . . . mediation of reconciliation with God."[34] In the context of harm, the creative Spirit that swept over the primal generative waters *can* bring about vitality without violence; the resurrection experience is the possibility that justice and mercy *can* embrace in the very context of suffering violence and injustice. When the desire for vitality and wellbeing bubbles up in the context of annihilating injustice, the sacred breath of creation is at work. The Spirit of God, symbolized by the wind and the breath in Genesis, transforms the victim, enveloped in and paralyzed by evil (suffering), into a free person endowed with newfound humanity, peace, and creativity (flourishing).

The language of resurrection is in sharp contrast to the scientific discourse of cause-effect-interventions; it is a language that engages the imagination. James Alison comments upon the specific

33. Robinette, *Grammars of Resurrection*, 362.
34. Robinette, *Grammars of Resurrection*, 362.

configuration of the human imagination that is required for such meaning-making. Jesus cultivated this kind of imagination and becomes our model.

> Jesus' imagination is absolutely possessed by God's deathless vivaciousness. Ours is not. . . .
>
> The access that we have to that deathless vivaciousness is by a slow opening of our imagination to that reality; that is what we understand by faith: the keeping open of our mind and imagination to the utter vivaciousness and deathlessness of God.

This type of openness of the mind was not possible for the philosophers of antiquity any more than it is accessible to the modern mindset of cause-effect explanations. Restricted to its own resources such as the empirical methodologies of science, the human mind can neither come up with nor figure out the divine vivaciousness and deathlessness that Jesus knew. God-as-deathless-vitality was and continues to be communicated to humankind experientially. It was the life and sayings of Jesus that called forth the human imagination of his disciples to something that previously had been inaccessible to the thinking mind. This calling forth of the human imagination to grope beyond the empiricism of death's ultimacy continues to impel the sufferer towards wellbeing and flourishing.

Those first witnesses of Jesus' death and resurrection had come to believe in him by experiencing the generous, loving person that he was. In experiencing his dying, they came face-to-face with something utterly mindboggling. Jesus was exercising neither sadomasochism nor violent vengeance, and it was certainly not the usual experience of a life defeated by suffering and death. In being raised from the dead, Jesus had created a new belief. "He was producing in his disciples a belief in the non-importance of death by passing through it himself in the first place to show that it is possible."[35] The resurrection experience had the effect then (as it does now) of reshaping experiences of suffering and death as "a non-definitive, non-toxic part of [one's] story."[36] And yet the experience of the vic-

---

35. Alison, *Raising Abel,* 61.
36. Alison, *Raising Abel,* 63.

tim immobilized by suffering is not rendered dispensible, invisible, or without value; it is by passing *through* the hurt, the immobilization, and the annihilation that the sufferer ultimately arrives at the state of flourishing. This mystery, if it is to be appropriated, requires the imagination to be configured in a very particular way. The unenlightened imagination sees God as "a paternity which kills and persecutes in order to serve 'god.'" By contrast, the one with "eyes to see and ears to hear"[37] recognizes "a paternity which is shown in the self-giving in the midst of violence as a witness to the complete vivaciousness of the God who knows no death."[38] Jesus modeled the possibility that the human interiority, with its sensibilities illumined, could bring a person *through* death into resurrection. When the imagination is thus configured, it becomes possible to experience the evil of affliction and even of death, while at the same time participating the divine subversion of that particular evil. The subversion of evil is a dynamic of resurrection, in which the sufferer advances stepwise into eternal wellbeing.

David Burrell has elaborated upon the freedom for this advance into wellness. He contends that our post-modern understanding of freedom is a libertarian version of freedom, which is nothing more than the freedom to do otherwise.[39] Freedom thus understood is about power dynamics that devolve into violence; the free agent is one who does what he/she wants to do. This kind of freedom readily becomes a discourse of ideologies such as the rights of "free choice." Focused exclusively upon ideas, without attention to discernment and the ordering of one's desires, "gratification and domination quickly fill the void in an account which had neglected the dynamics of desire from the outset."[40] When the subversion of evil is viewed as nothing more than an exercise in the dynamics of coercion to gratify the person in power, true flourishing does not come about. "Failing to advert to the dynamics of our desires

---

37. Jesus said, "For judgment I came into this world, that those who do not see may see, and that those who see may become blind." (John 9:39; see also Ezek 40:4; 44:5; Rom 11:8).

38. Alison, *Raising Abel,* 65.

39. Burrell, *Learning to Trust,* 1.

40. Burrell, *Learning to Trust,* 4.

simply invites self-deception regarding the freedom of our actions, since 'what we wanna do' seldom originates from our very selves, and is usually elicited by multiple (and often powerfully presented) enticements, to which we are ever vulnerable."[41] Burrell holds that it is the absence or denial of a telos that culminates in "unabashedly [using] our freedom to promote our own gratification."[42]

In the context of this essay on attending the sufferer, if the resurrection dynamic of flourishing became our rediscovered telos, then a new understanding of freedom would evolve. The freedom of a resurrection dynamic is not adequately described as an intellectual choice between good and evil. Nor is it the freedom of modernity that feels entitled to deploy every possible intervention towards restoring the norms of physiology, culture, and morality. When flourishing is understood as a resurrection dynamic then freedom becomes experiential—the experience of suffering and annihilation subverted. In other words, flourishing hinges on the good towards which one perseveres, and not on a resolution of suffering.

When viewed from below, the resurrection dynamic that perseveres towards wellbeing in the context of suffering arises within the sensory nature. To participate the subversion of suffering is highly dependent upon a process of scrutiny of the evils—the hurts, paralyses, and silencings—that have imprinted themselves upon the sensory interiority. While it longs to flourish, the sensory nature is hindered by these negative experiences. From above, one might conclude that such necessary scrutiny is an exercise in the willed endurance of sensory suppression. But from below, the scrutiny is a practiced habit of experiencing ever-increasing sacred animation whereby the appetitions arising from hurt towards false goods (e.g., vengeance) are ultimately displaced by new longings arising within a re-configured, healing interiority (e.g., forgiveness). The experiences of sacred animation are mundane daily experiences: a bright sunny day, a robin on the lawn, the fragrance of a rose, a baby's laugh, a phone call from one's friend, etc. The choice is in the apprehension of these mundane experiences as life-giving. It is this

41. Burrell, *Learning to Trust,* 7.
42. Burrell, *Learning to Trust,* 4.

(graced) sensory apprehension that subverts the torpor and apathy of suffering and brings about revitalized capacities of appetition. On this view, the resurrection dynamic is a chosen response to the *experience* of suffering, and contrasts with the prevailing imperative to respond with a solution to the *problem* of suffering. Wellbeing is not suffering-fixed but is rather an instantiation of the ineffable resurrection dynamic of suffering-subverted.

Burrell contrasts the logic that tries to make sense of things and the conviction that there is a sense to it all. The former is possibly the problem-solving, analytical kind of logic, whereas the latter is perhaps this immersion in the meaningful sensibilities of lived experience. When suffering is reduced to an intellectual cognate, stripped of the sensory experience, the mind pursues suffering as a problem requiring an intervention and a solution. On that view, a solution to the problem of suffering causes the effect of flourishing. This cause-effect-intervention approach is what Burrell calls an explanatory paradigm. He points out that a non-explanatory approach points in an alternate direction. This alternate paradigm is "a language into which we are called to enter if we would allow our life to become a journey. And the promise of undertaking such a journey is not only sense or direction for our lives, but also a sense for it all."[43] Suffering is by its very definition paralyzing and overwhelming;[44] it is hard to make logical sense of suffering. But in the view from below, we see that the sensory corporeality is equipped to respond to adversity because it is allured by animation and it avoids annihilation. These primal sensibilities equip the sufferer for the journey that little-by-little makes sense of it all.

In this section, flourishing has been described as suffering-subverted. On this view, flourishing is a resurrection dynamic. Flourishing as a resurrection dynamic challenges the imagination to proceed without the usual problem-solving analyses and to work instead with symbol and metaphor. The resurrection narratives reveal the possibility of subverting our experiences of annihilation with immersion into the life-giving mundane. Flourishing does

43. Burrell, *Learning to Trust*, 45.
44. See chapter 1 above.

not depend upon a resolution of suffering but upon a heightened awareness of vitality. The appetite or longing for life intensifies and becomes more nuanced in proportion to the acuity of one's awareness of life-giving experiences. The freedom from problem-solving is associated with the freedom for an experiential immersion in that sensed gradient from annihilation towards eternal animation.

SUMMARY

The movement from suffering to flourishing is founded upon an experience of freedom for intimacy with the divine Being who is pure *actus*. Such intimacy affords a progressive capacity to participate the supreme movement (*actus*) of aliveness (being). Flourishing, thus understood, defies the empirical, endless cycles of destruction so logically beyond doubt. On this non-secular view, flourishing is an arduous experience of subversion of the hurts and annihilations of suffering. Flourishing is that ineffable dynamic of the resurrection, experienced at the level of the sensory nature as "the sense of it all," a kind of meaning whereby life is understood without reference to death, in defiance of all explanatory logic. At the level of sensory experience, flourishing is that which lies beyond suffering and death, namely, the experience of participating divine aliveness. Using the linguistic tools of symbol and metaphor, the narrative of the sufferer describes an ineffable, sacred journey of transformation towards flourishing. On this view, suffering is a state of being stuck in immobility or even in invisibility (non-existence); it is associated with the feeling sense of being cut off from participating divine aliveness, stuck in overwhelming feelings of doom and impending annihilation. Suffering progressing inexorably towards the immobility of a corpse is loudly prophesied by the cause-effect logic of our secular empiricism as the ultimate and only human destiny; in our discourse of moral principles, the same logic of cause-effect prophesies condemnation for those who deviate from the perceived norms. But if suffering and flourishing could be re-imagined—and desired—as experiential aspects of the ineffable, then a different narrative would become possible. On this view, contemplation becomes key. The disciplined stance or arduous posture that is contemplation enables a progressive transformation of the immobility of bondage into the stillness of waiting attentively for the beloved. Contemplation involves a corporeal sensory experience (meaning hard work, unpleasant feelings, arduous recollections, anything-but-easy, etc) of receptivity to the ineffable that leads ultimately into the joy-filled, no-more-hurts kind of life that the tradition has called resurrection. To live the resurrection is to participate the divine Being in whom there is no death—no corpse-like immobility—at all, in whom there is only life, vitality, and dynamism in its fullest. To participate life in its fullest is to find an eternal resting place for the scars of all hurts and annihilations, certain that no power, no logic, and no violence on earth can ever re-open those wounds that previously hindered the flourishing.

5

Concluding Statements

A smoker knows, at the intellectual level, that, in general, smok-ing causes cancer and death, but his *experience* of pleasure—a release from anxiety, a sense of felt ease, a certain social camaraderie, etc.—reinforces the bad habit. In order to change the harmful habit that smoking is, the paradigm of cause-effect, with its proofs and arguments, is inadequate. I have endeavored to introduce a comple-mentary paradigm more suited to the pursuit of a felt sense of well-being, one which proceeds from a starting point of experiences of un-wellness or suffering. The specifications of this proposed para-digm are not "out there" awaiting our discovery by critical analyses; this new paradigm is rather a heuristic that unfolds experientially "from within." Rather than arising from empirical deductions, it aggregates from lived experiences into a kind of wisdom around suffering and wellbeing, i.e., around evil and good. To indicate the analytic empirical logic I have used the term, "from above," and for the experiential wisdom, I have used the term, "from below." The paradigm "from below" places emphasis upon one's movement in response to experiences of hurt and harm, experiences that can-not be eradicated or "fixed" by abstraction and speculation. If he

81

is to advance towards wellbeing, the smoker—indeed anyone with a harmful habit—must first immerse himself in and heal from those physically sensed hurts of his past. A person of modernity is tempted to "think of" the hurts in terms of psychology, physiology, and the various pathologies, but for the medieval Thomas Aquinas, one's corporeality was not the stage where science played itself out and restored one to the state of being normal. Thomas was after sanctity. He understood the sensory nature—the body—as the locus of felt experiences of woundedness, inflicted by such evils as injustice, violence, greed, etc. It is these imprints of evil that find their expression in desires seduced by false goods. We might understand smoking as an instance of one such alluring but false good. In other words, when we take the perspective from below, we recognize that our human corporeality is *vulnerable* to evil, and evil allures under the guise of some false good. In a previous era, when the prevailing view was from above, one spoke of human corporeality as *culpable* for such destructive habits as, for example, smoking. Until now, vulnerability has been (at best) an after-*thought* but most certainly not an *experience* with any moral or spiritual significance.

If the emphasis were to shift and grant moral validity to experiences of the one who is suffering on account of vulnerability to hurt, how would our use of language change? Our Western culture has been critiqued for enabling an empowered observer to adjudicate and to penalize the one who falls outside the law, a paradigm that intentionally inflicts suffering, justifying and often sacralizing such oppression in the name of pursuing the good. In this prevailing paradigm, good and evil as well as flourishing and suffering have become cognates, abstracted from the experience of the one who is being objectified, observed, adjudicated, and penalized. It is an heuristic that sees from above and that uses language shaped by logic: if this, then that must follow. Ours is a paradigm of cause and effect, shaped by the critical analytical capacities of the intellectual nature. But if we opt for the poor, the sick, and the disenfranchised—in short, for the sufferer—then the language of logic becomes insufficient because it leaves out the *experience* of both the sufferer and the observing thinker. I have suggested that a language ordered to the voice of the sufferer will take the form of narrative. Narrative is suitable because it privileges the power of the ineffable with no need to de-mystify suffering. The language of mystery—of suffering—makes use of symbols and metaphors, not syllogisms and proofs. The language of symbolism with which one communicates the ineffable, experiential dimension of suffering is hortatory rather than persuasive in its impact. It calls forth in the (former) observer-thinker a movement (as opposed to a thought) in response to the narrative of a sufferer; in other words, the listener is now moved by the teller's story—and that subjectivity is OK! This non-cognitive, responsive movement is an immersion in the bodily felt-sense of the hurt. To be moved by another amounts to an experience of immersion into one's own sensory interiority. With one's sensory nature aroused one experiences suffering vicariously as the teller reveals her own experiences of hurt and harm.

When confronted with a moral dilemma, whether in medical ethics or in social ethics, the deliberations often intend to reflect dispositions of compassion and humane-ness towards the sufferer. But just how to integrate compassion into a debate that recognizes as legitimate only the language of proofs, evidence, and logic has until now remained unspecified. In the preceding pages I have introduced a paradigm intended to complement our logic-driven scientific discourses of modernity. This new paradigm is better suited to communicating the *experiences* of the sufferer. When lived experiences (rather than ideas) gain legitimacy, then there is less need to communicate in abstract universal statements.

The proposed new paradigm is founded (prayerfully) upon both my experience as a physician and my doctoral research into the texts of Thomas Aquinas and others from the Christian tradition of theology/philosophy. Despite the appalling harm perpetrated by historical deviations from these traditions of healing, both medicine and Christianity have traditionally cultivated a disposition of attending the sufferer from sickness into wellbeing and from bondage into freedom. I would hope that the reader of these pages might be inspired to explore their own faith traditions and professional roles so as to further define and clarify this emerging new paradigm around physically experienced movements. Then, when our moral dilemmas move beyond cigarette/substance addictions to abortion, euthanasia, genetic modification, etc., not only will we be able to understand the abstract ideas that are true in general, but we will also have a felt sense of the complex desires of a sufferer. These complex desires of the sufferer are conveyed as both the emergence into a freedom for flourishing and a stuck-ness in the paralyses of suffering. The new paradigm will work with a language of symbolism around suffering (evil) and flourishing (good) that will be complementary to the logic of the universally true. This new paradigm will serve to reveal and to illumine an important aspect of reality that is unaccounted for by the cause-effect logic of science. This is the aspect of reality that is felt at a deeply visceral level when attending the sufferer. And the sufferer is she who lives not only in our midst but also deep within the self.

Bibliography

Alison, James. *Raising Abel: The Recovery of the Eschatological Imagination.* New York: Crossroad, 2003.

Andrews, Arin. *Some Assembly Required: The Not So Secret Life of a Transgender Teen.* New York: Simon and Schuster, 2014.

Anscombe, G. E. M. *Intention.* Cambridge, MA: Harvard University Press, 1957.

Bader-Saye, Scott. "The Transgender Body's Grace." *Journal of the Society of Christian Ethics* 39.1 (2019) 75–92.

Botha, Elaine. *Metaphor and Its Moorings: Studies in the Grounding of Metaphorical Meaning.* New York: Peter Lang, 2007.

Burrell, David B. *Learning to Trust in Freedom: Signs from Jewish, Christian, and Muslim Traditions.* Scranton, PA: University of Scranton Press, 2010.

Campbell, Peter A., and Edwin M. McMahon. *Bio-Spirituality: Focusing as a Way to Grow.* Chicago: Loyola University Press, 1985.

Cassell, Eric J. *The Nature of Suffering and the Goals of Medicine.* 2nd ed. New York: Oxford University Press, 2004.

Cates, Diana Fritz. *Aquinas on Emotions: A Religious Ethical Inquiry.* Washington, DC: Georgetown University Press, 2009.

Charon, Rita. *Narrative Medicine: Honoring the Stories of Illness.* New York: Oxford University Press, 2006.

Charon, Rita, and Laurie Zoloth. "Like an Open Book: Reliability, Intersubjectivity, and Textuality in Bioethics." In *Stories Matter: The Role of Narrative in Medical Ethics,* edited by Rita Charon and Martha Montello, 21–36. New York: Routledge, 2002.

Coakley, Sarah. *God, Sexuality, and the Self: An Essay on the Trinity.* Cambridge: Cambridge University Press, 2013.

DeHaan, Daniel D. "Perception and the Vis Cogitativa: A Thomistic Analysis of Aspectual, Actual, and Affectional Percepts." *American Catholic Philosophical Quarterly* 88.3 (2014) 397–437.

Dodds, Michael J. "Caring for Girls and Women Who Are Considering Abortion: Rethinking Informed Consent." In *Medicine and the Ethics of Care*, edited by Diana Fritz Cates and Paul Lauritzen, 162–203. Moral Traditions and Moral Arguments Series. Washington, DC: Georgetown University Press, 2001.

———. "Thomas Aquinas, Human Suffering, and the Unchanging God of Love." *Theological Studies* 52 (1991) 330–44.

Frank, Arthur W. *The Wounded Story-Teller: Body, Illness, and Ethics.* Chicago: University of Chicago Press, 1995.

Girard, René. *I See Satan Fall Like Lightning.* Translated by James C. Williams. Mayknoll, NY: Orbis, 2002.

Gondreau, Paul. *The Passions of Christ's Soul in the Theology of St Thomas Aquinas.* Scranton, PA: University of Scranton Press, 2009.

Grisez, Germain. "The First Principle of Practical Reason; A Commentary on the Summa Theologiae, 1–2, Question 94, Article 2." *Natural Law Forum* 10.1 (1965) 168–201.

Hall, M. Elizabeth Lewis, et al. "The Role of Suffering in Human Flourishing: Contributions from Positive Psychology, Theology, and Philosophy." *Journal of Psychology and Theology* 38.2 (2010) 111–21.

Hudson Jones, Anne. "Literature and Medicine: Narrative Ethics." *Lancet* 349 (1997) 1243–46.

John Paul II. *Veritatis Splendor.* Encyclical given August 6, 1993. Online. http://www.vatican.va/content/john-paul-ii/en/encyclicals/documents/hf_jp-ii_enc_06081993_veritatis-splendor.html.

Laidlaw, Micheal K., et al. "Endocrine Treatment of Gender-Dysphoric/Gender-Incongruent Persons: An Endocrine Society Clinical Practice Guideline." *J Clin Endocrinol Metab* 104.3 (2019) 686–87.

Lewis, Bradley. "Narrative Medicine and Contemplative Care at the End of Life." *Journal of Religion and Health* 55 (2016) 309–24.

MacIntyre, Alasdair. *After Virtue: A Study in Moral Theory.* 3rd ed. London: Bristol Classical, 2011.

———. *Ethics and the Conflicts of Modernity: An Essay on Desire, Practical Reasoning, and Narrative.* Cambridge: Cambridge University Press, 2016.

Martel, Yann. *The High Mountains of Portugal.* Toronto: Knopf Canada, 2016.

Milbank, John. "What Liberal Intellectuals Get Wrong about Transgenderism." *Catholic Herald*, January 13, 2017.

Miner, Robert. *Thomas Aquinas on the Passions.* Cambridge: Cambridge University Press, 2009.

O'Donovan, Oliver. "Transexualism and Christian Marriage." *Journal of Religious Ethics* 11.1 (1983) 143.

Pasnau, Robert. *Thomas Aquinas on Human Nature: A Philosophical Study of Summa Theologiae Ia 75–89.* Cambridge: University of Cambridge Press, 2002.

Pinckaers, Servais-Théodore. "Scripture and the Renewal of Moral Theology." In *The Pinckaers Reader: Renewing Thomistic Moral Theology,* by Servais-Théodore Pinckaers, 46–63. Washington, DC: Catholic University of America, 2005.

Puhl, Louis J. *The Spiritual Exercises of St Ignatius, Based upon Studies in the Langauge of the Autograph.* Chicago: Loyola University Press, 1951.

Rhonheimer, Martin. "Is Christian Morality Reasonable? On the Difference Between Secular and Christian Humanism." In *The Perspective of the Acting Person: Essays in the Renewal of Thomistic Moral Philosophy,* edited by William F. Murphy Jr., 1–17. Washington, DC: Catholic University Press of America, 2008.

———. "Practical Reason and the Naturally Rational." In *The Persepctive of the Acting Person: Essays in the Renewal of Thomistic Moral Philosophy,* edited by William F. Murphy Jr., 95–128. Washington, DC: Catholic University of America Press, 2008.

Robinette, Brian. *Grammars of Resurrection: A Christian Theology of Presence and Absence.* New York: Crossroad, 2009.

Rosenbaum, Lisa. "Being Like Mike—Fear, Trust, and the Tragic Death of Michael Davidson." *New England Journal of Medicine* 372 (2015) 798–99.

Shaer, Matthew. "The Long Lonely Road of Chelsea Manning." *New York Times Magazine,* June 12, 2017. Online. http://www.nytimes.com/2017/06/12/magazine/the-long-lonely-road-of-chelsea-manning.html.

Soelle, Dorothee. *Suffering.* Translated by Everett R. Kalin. Philadelphia: Fortress, 1975.

Thomas Aquinas. *Summa Theologica.* Translated by Fathers of the English Dominican Province. Complete English ed. 5 vols. Notre Dame, IN: Ave Maria, 1920.

Williams, Rowan. *The Body's Grace.* Edited by Eugene G. Rogers Jr. Oxford: Blackwell, 2002.

Index

human desiring, acquiring moral
  nuance, 71
human dynamic, of emergence
  from suffering, 3
human existence, aspect of mystery
  in, 41
human experience, retaining
  suffering as, 25
human flourishing, as a reference
  point for MacIntyre, 33
human interiority, 24, 28, 43, 76.
  See also interiority
human longing, for release, xxi
human misery, as the experiential
  matrix, 34
human movements, elevated to
  moral agency, 38
human nature
  as permeable to the good and
    to the hurts, 10
  as the sensory body moving,
    45–46
  Thomas Aquinas on the dual
    capacities of, 21
  understanding illumined by
    theology, 1
human sensory movement, at a
  symbolic level, 26
humanities, enabling the helping
  professional, 40
hurt, healing from recurrent
  experiences of, 58
hurt (evil), sensory nature
  responding to, 8
hurt and harm, shaping the self as
  sufferer, 9
hurt or hindrance, shaping
  movements, 10
hurtful objects, deceptive allure
  of, 8
hurting, not synonymous with
  being wrong, 68

ideas and principles, in the first
  case presentation, 51
Ignatian tradition of spirituality, 71
illegitimacy, experience of, 73
image, 7
imagination, 7, 74, 75, 76
immaterial cognitions and
    abstractions, intellectual
    nature of, xxi
immaterial soul, disturbance of, 8
immobility and muteness, bondage
  of, 9
immobilization and silencing,
  experience of, 38
"impediments," to flourishing, 27
imperatives of power over another,
  avoiding, xxi
imprints
  configuring, 7
  of evil, 82
  of evil-as-hurt, 4
  with intrinsic meanings, 30
  of lived experiences, 28, 52
indigenous woman patient, 2, 18
the ineffable
  in clinical discourse, 39–56
  experience of, 41, 44
innate "smarts," 6
inner sensibilities, applied by the
  self, 63
instinct, in animals, 6, 61
"intake histories," 21, 40
intellect
  analytic, 21
  conscious of sensory nature, 61
  of intellectual nature, 6
  irascible passions arising
    independently of, 8
  problem-solving, 9
  Thomas privileging the
    working of, 3
intellectual nature, 57–58, 61
intelligence, unique to sensory
  nature, 5–6

medicine, 46, 71n27

"medium of becoming," narrative
offering, 43

memory, internal sense of, 28

mendacity, problem-solving
intellect disoriented by, 9

metanarrative
of becoming well, 35, 36, 37,
53–54, 55, 56
complementary guiding ethics,
32
of the true-in-general, 34, 51,
54, 55

metaphors, in the second case
presentation, 54

methodology, from above vs from
below, 65

Milbank, John, 66, 67

Miner, Robert, 7

misery, as particular experiences, 34

Modern Moral Philosophy
(Anscombe), 23

modernity
bias of the critical mind of, 3
opposition between religion
and science, 2
overcoming evidence-based
claims of, 58
political, 60
truth confounded in, 24
view for above as default, 18

moral absolutes, 31

moral act, 31

moral agency. *See also* agency
born in process of the telling, xx
human movements elevated
to, 38
risk of escalating suffering, 22
sufferers robbed of, 12

moral awareness, from below, 69

moral becoming, 37

moral discernment, 65

moral discourse, used in stating
Objections, 67

moral good, in the expressivist
paradigm, 33

moral imperative, 10, 31, 50

moral life, shifting from misery
into beatitude, 34

Moral Manuals, tradition of, 34

moral movement, as particular, 31

moral observer, contrast with the
sufferer, 66

moral reasoning, 34

moral tension, 22–23, 69. *See also*
tension

moral validity, of experiences of
the sufferer, 82

morality, of erotic desire, 69

movement(s)
describing an experience of,
25–26
discourse of, xix
facilitator identifying, 53
from the false good towards
the true good, 17
guided by know-how, 23
as intrinsic to being human, 5
researching through
scholarship, 22
in the sensory nature, 5–9
from suffering to flourishing,
79
Thomas Aquinas on, 21–38
towards the good, xxi

mundane experiences, as life-
giving, 77–78

murder, 45

music-making, 30, 31

mute victims, 18

mystery
communicating around, 54
dialogue around in real life, 53
language of, 83
in the second case
presentation, 54
suffering as, 42–47

physicians, easily rendered mute
and paralyzed, xxii
pianist, expressing movements of
his passions, 30
Pinckaers, Servais-Théodore, 32,
34–35
pleasure
distinction from flourishing, 42
ensuring safety from harm, 5
movement following a gradient
of hurt and, 15
smokers experiencing, 81
power dynamics, devolving into
violence, 76
power of symbol, xx
practical ethics, foundational
paradigm for, 21–38
practical experience, 15
practical principles, belonging to
synderesis, 17
practical rationality, 18
practical reason, 13–19, 23–24, 27.
See also reason
pregnancy, as an experience, 52
pre-modern understanding of
human nature, 41
Presence, experiencing, 44
primal intelligence, wanting to
emerge, 19
primal knowing, of the sensory
nature, 28
primal meanings, of harm or good
carried by images, 7
primal peace, arriving at, 74
primal sensibilities, equipping the
sufferer, 78
principles
in the first case presentation, 51
first practical, 64
moral, 69
naturally known judging
things, 17
of practical reason (percepts of
natural law), 15

universally true, xxi
principles-in-question, 66
problem-solving, de-emphasized
in the second case
presentation, 54
problem-solving suffering, 43–44
process of the telling, moral agency
born in, xx
prudence, 13–14, 14n20
psychology, 10, 51
psycho-somatic dysfunctionalities,
53
punishments, 63
pure *actus*, divine Being as, 79

Raj Quartet (Scott), 68
rationality
of action, 23–24
called forth by sensory nature,
14
ordered towards movement,
not cognition, 16
practical, 18
primal, 61
of sensory nature, xix, 19, 27
sensory nature awakening, 36
storied, xx
syllogistic, 14
symbolic, 62
reactive passions, 31
reality, of the sufferer, xvii
reason. *See also* practical reason
particular, 7, 61
as practical know-how, 16
of sensory nature, 6
speculative, 15, 17
reflective process, of practical
reason, 16
resting in the good attained,
movement of, 58
resurrection
dynamic of, 73, 77, 78
flourishing, soul-filled body
of, 74

view from below (continued)
  experiences remaining in the
    body, xx
  focusing on vulnerability to
    annihilation, 13
  on lived experience as a
    narrative, 61
  questing for the good as, xvii
  retaining the experience of
    suffering, xviii
  revealing an advancing into
    freedom, 71
  seeing apprehension as an
    experiential process, 16
  on sensory corporeality
    responding to adversity, 78
  synderesis as linguistic groping
    into contingency, 65
  understanding appetition in
    terms of the passions, 8
  working with dysphoria/
    suffering, 69
  Zoloth taking, 36
violence, 12, 45, 51, 76
visceral feeling-experiences, of a
  sensory nature, 36
visceral feelings, in the second case
  presentation, 54
visceral knowing, 37
visceral movement, 23
visceral resonance, xx, 51, 65
visceral responsiveness, 46
visceral sensibilities, engaging the
  listener, 40
vitality, 53, 56, 62, 79
vivaciousness, of the God who
  knows no death, 76
voice
  from below, 70

expressing inward thought and
  desire, 11
vulnerability, 12, 13n19, 15, 82
vulnerable inner self, dialogue with
  the competent executive
  self, 52
vulnerable seeker, advancing
  towards the good, 32

"wanting" and "good," connexion
  between, 7
wellbeing
  after a restored alignment with
    universal norms, 55
  consequence of a suffering-free
    state of, 10–11
  eternal, 18
  experience of obstruction of, 9
  finding within harm and
    annihilation, 45
  as not suffering-fixed, 78
  sensory nature responding to
    experiences of, 8
  soul's longing to be loved into,
    73
  struggle with obstacles or
    threats to, 60
wellness, human beings moved to
  pursue, 60
wellness and health, enabling
  flourishing, 9
wellness and hurt, felt experiences
  of, 28
Western culture, enabling an
  empowered observer, 82
Williams, Rowan, 68
wisdom, privileged over
  propositional logic, 34

Zoloth, Laurie, 36

www.ingramcontent.com/pod-product-compliance
Lightning Source LLC
Chambersburg PA
CBHW060311100426

42812CB00003B/743